Elephant Coloring Book

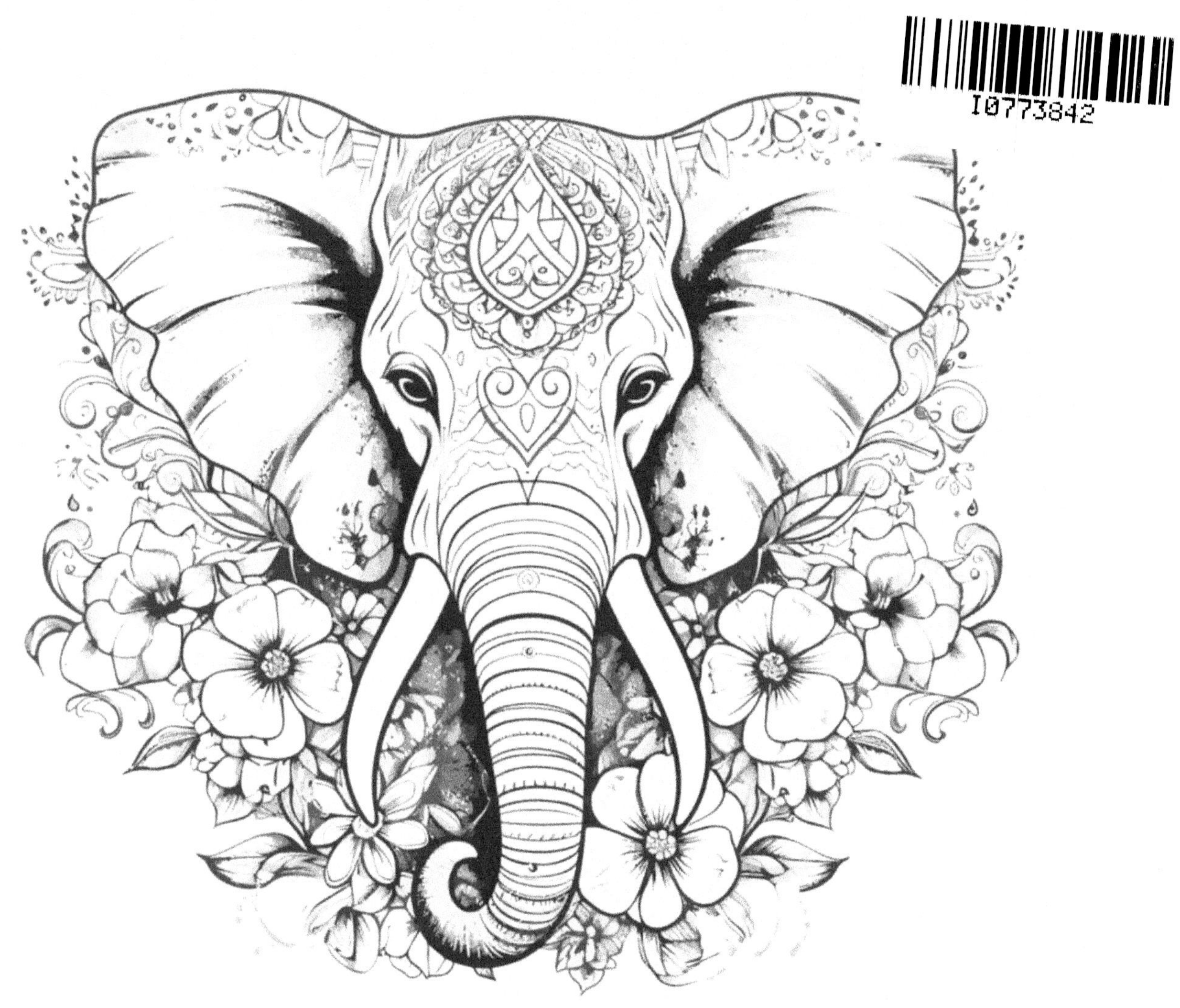

This Book Belongs To

....

....

....

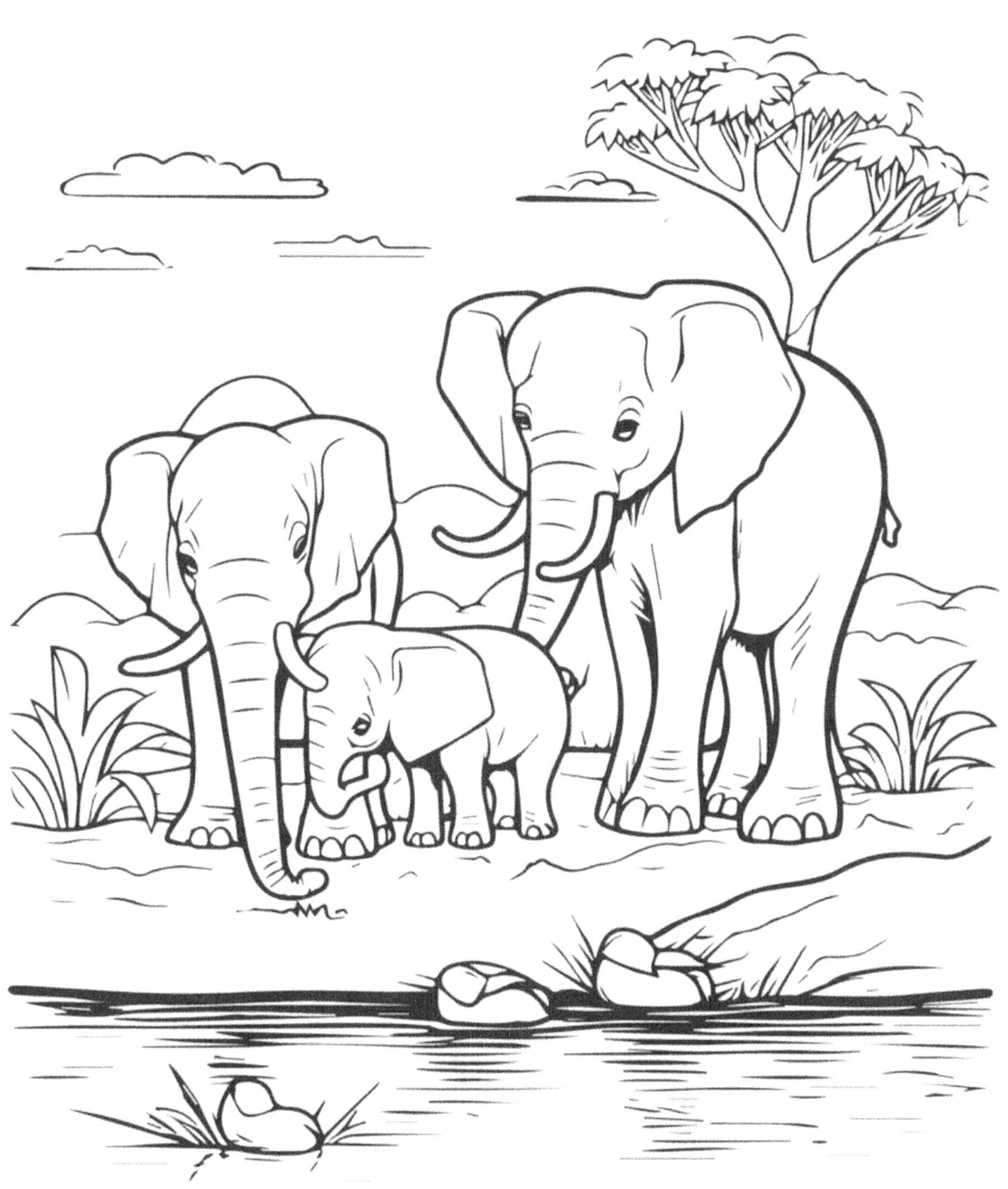

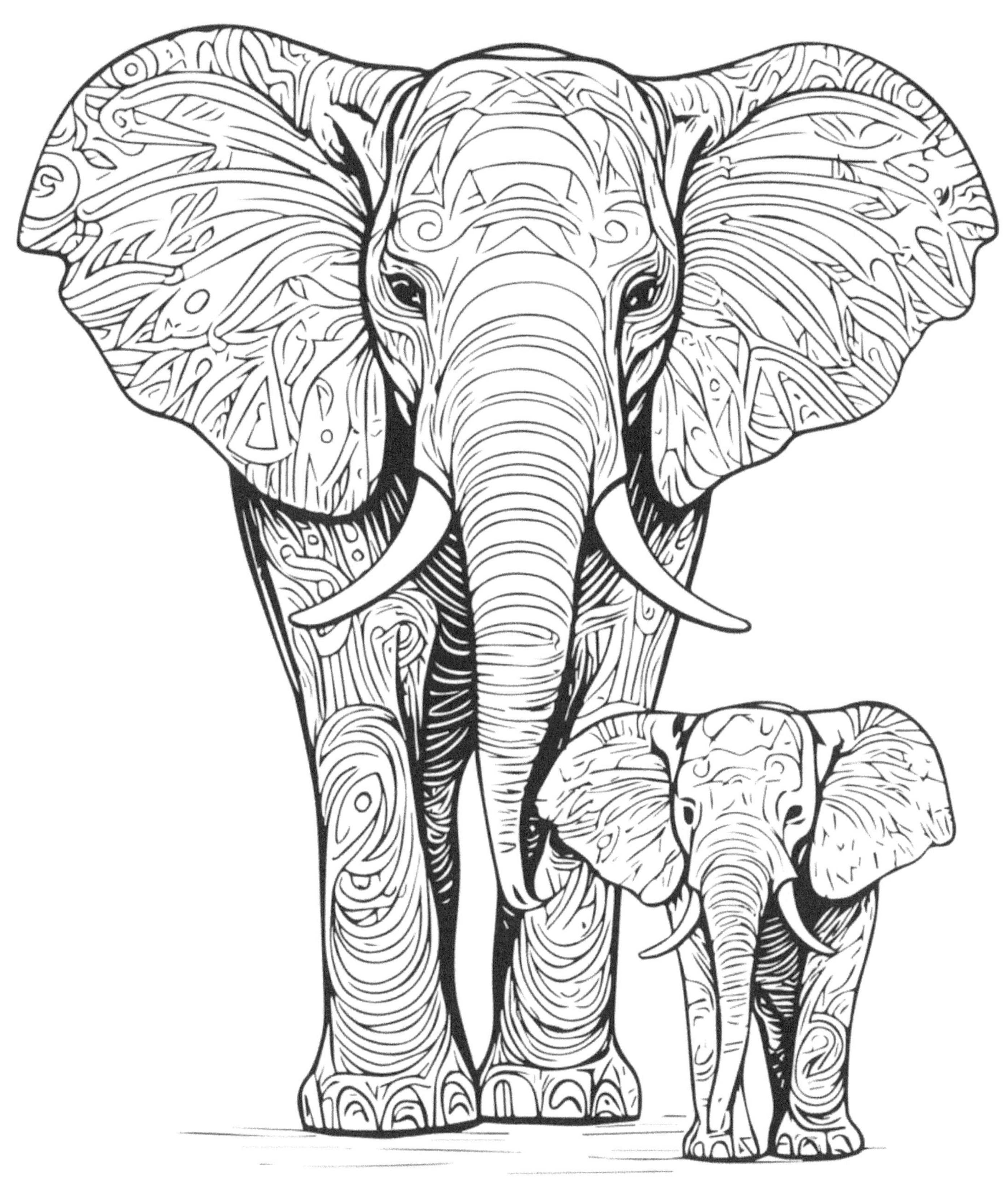

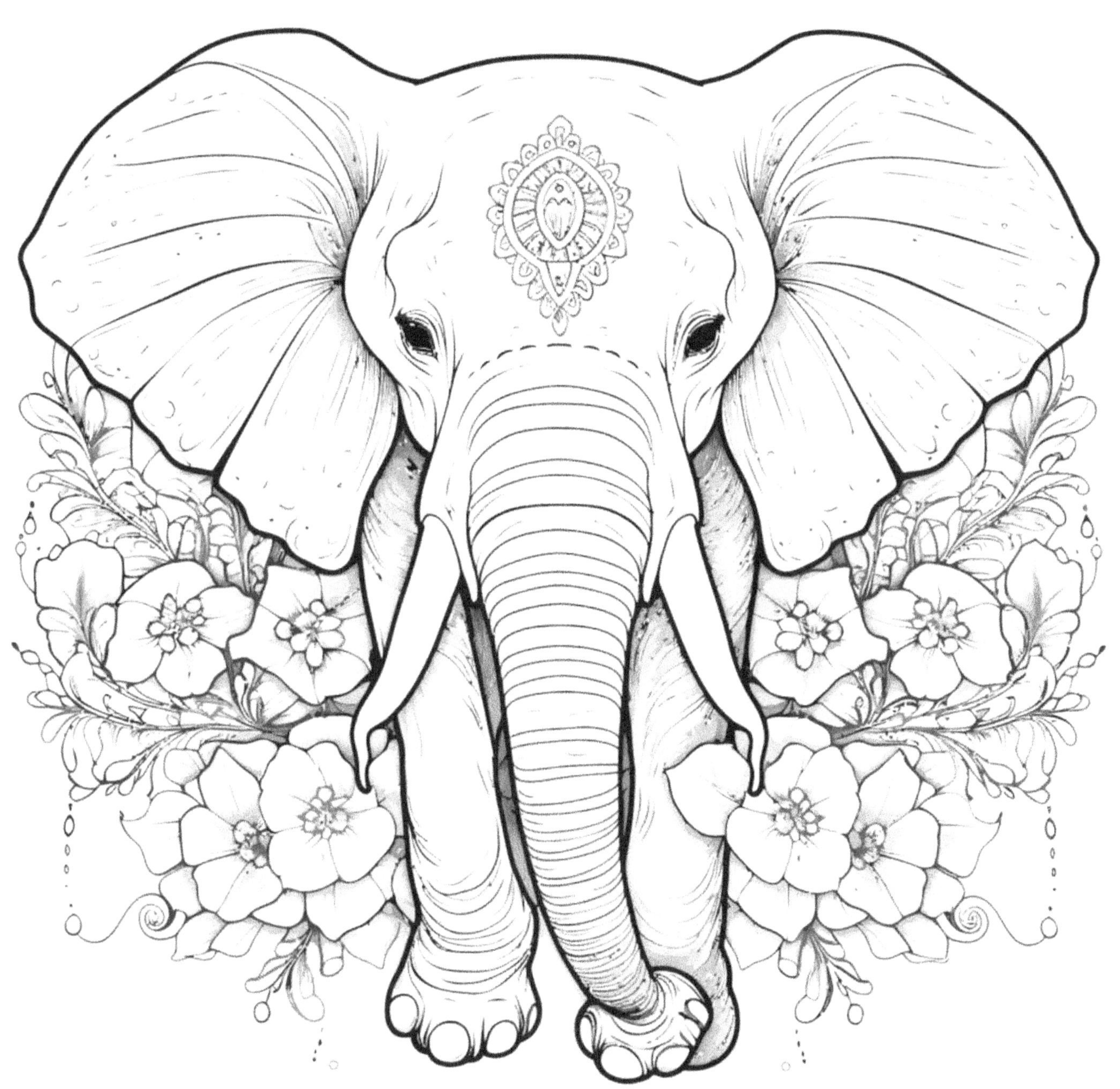

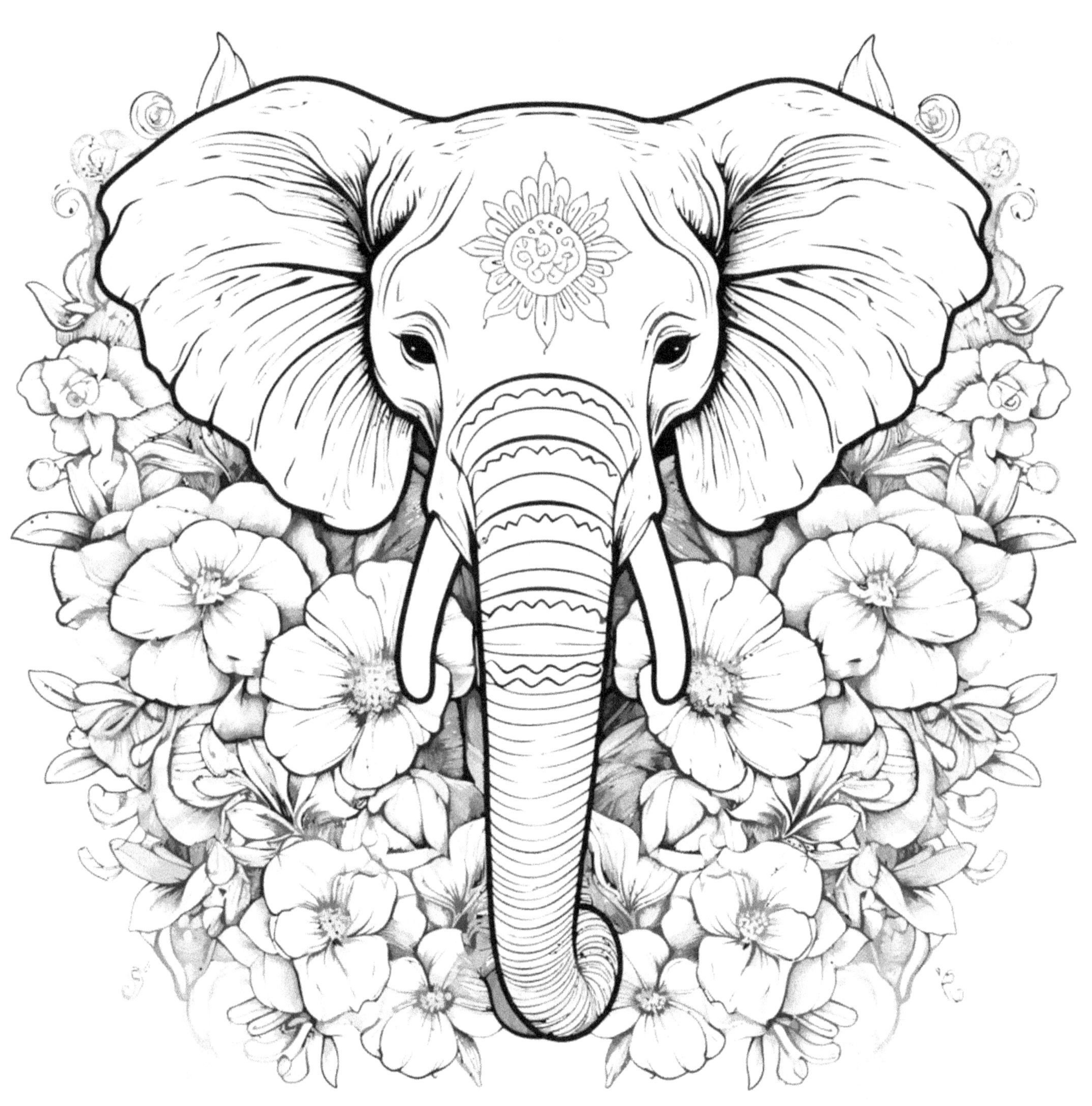

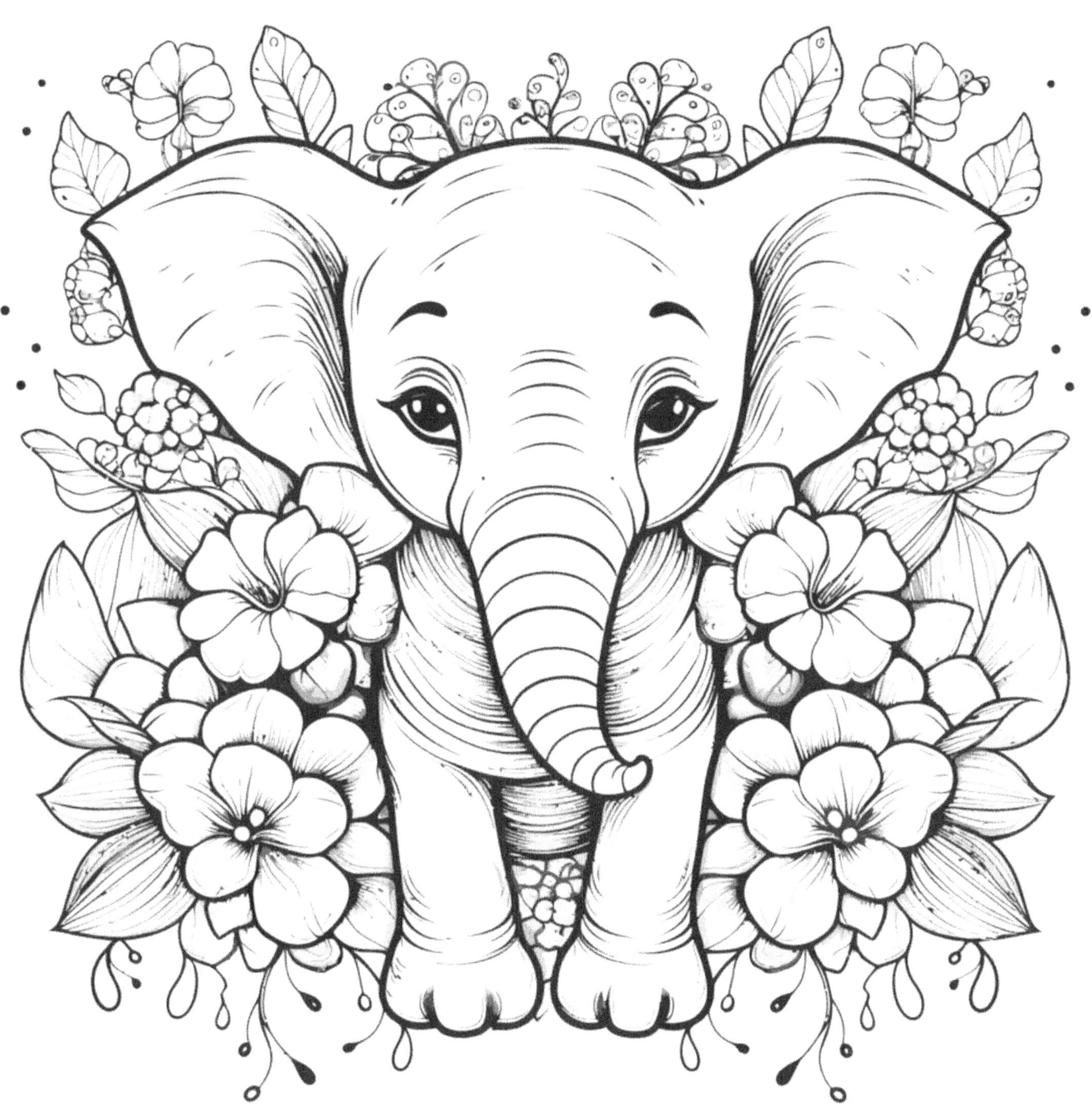

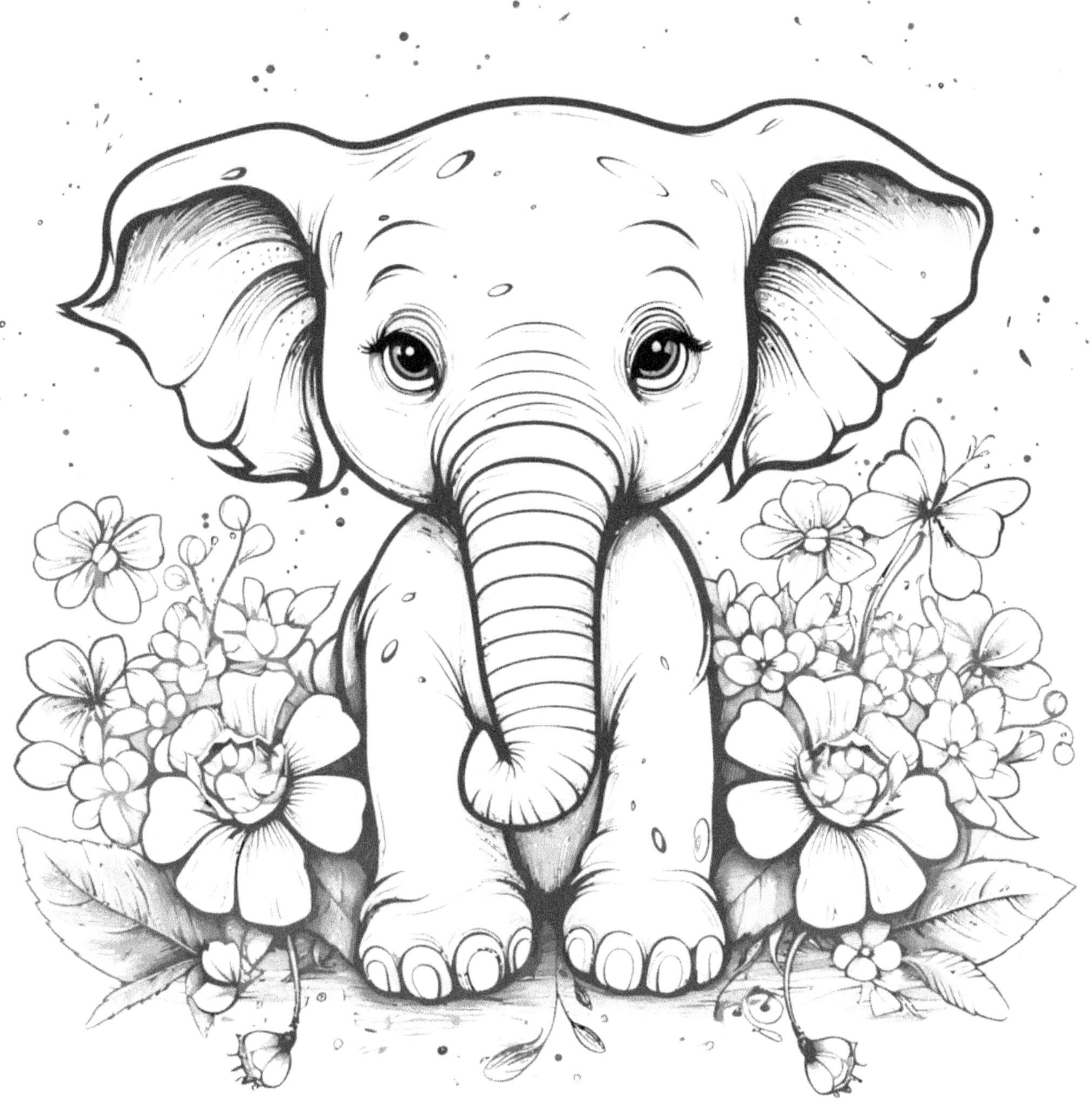

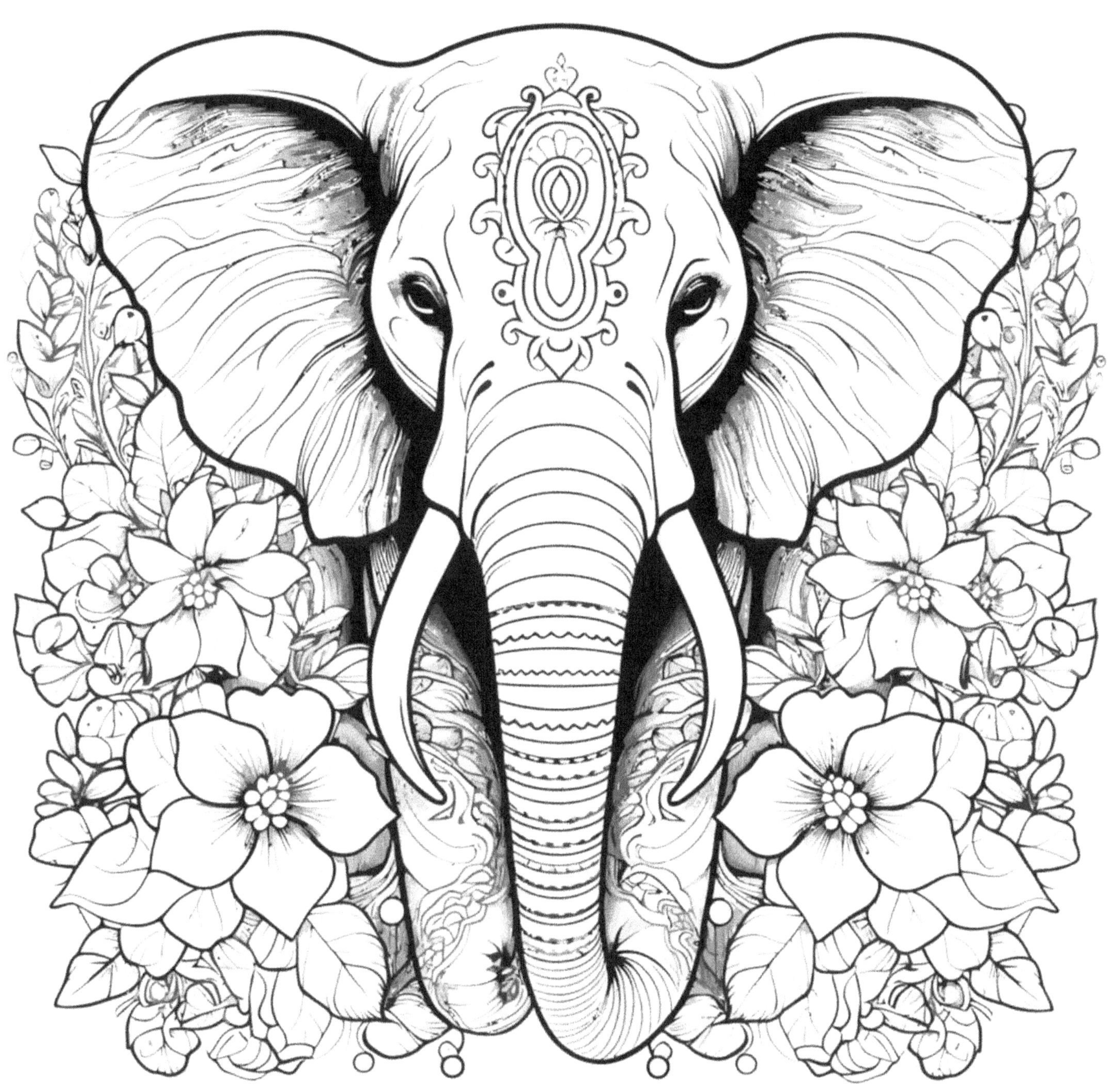

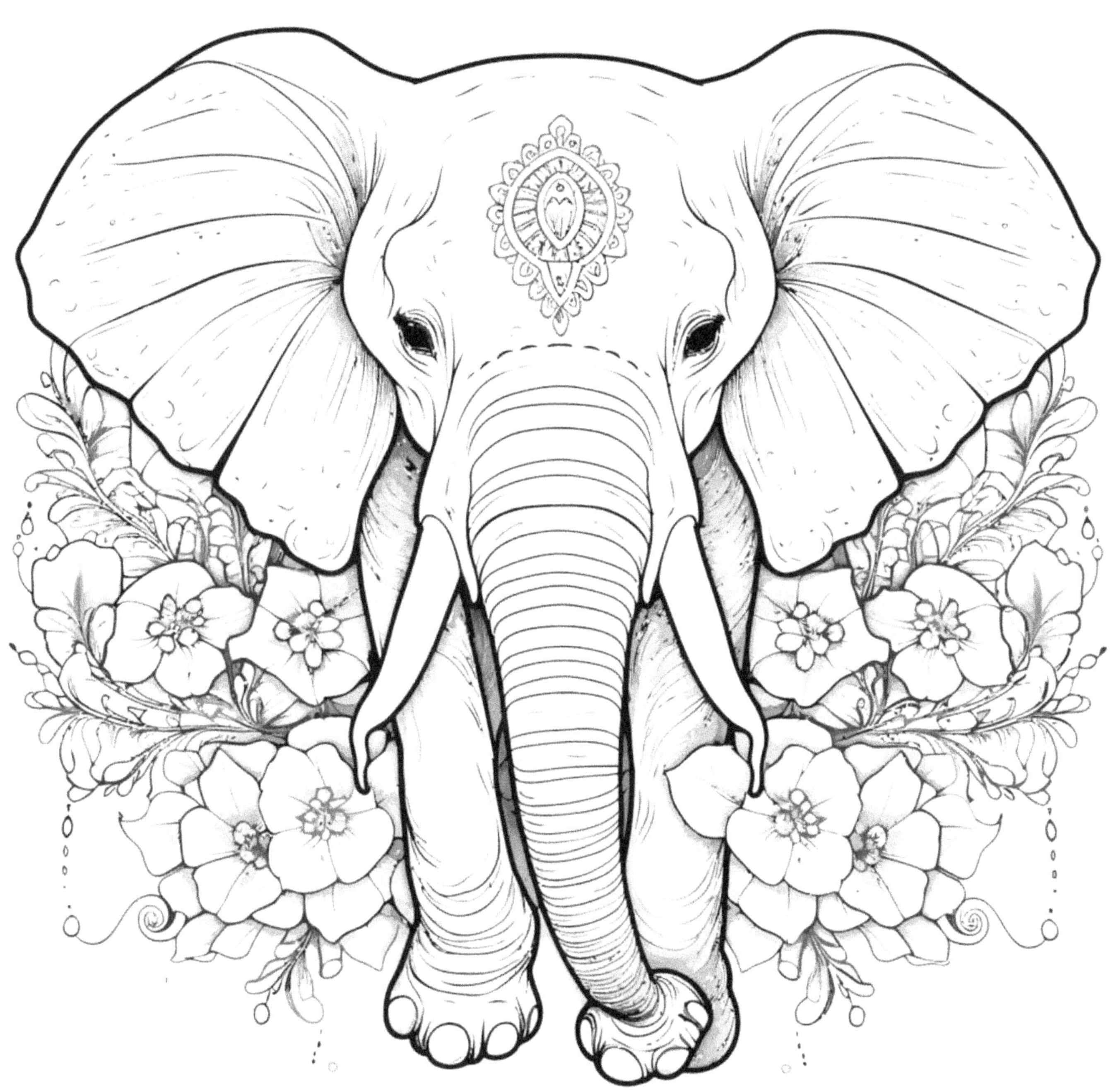

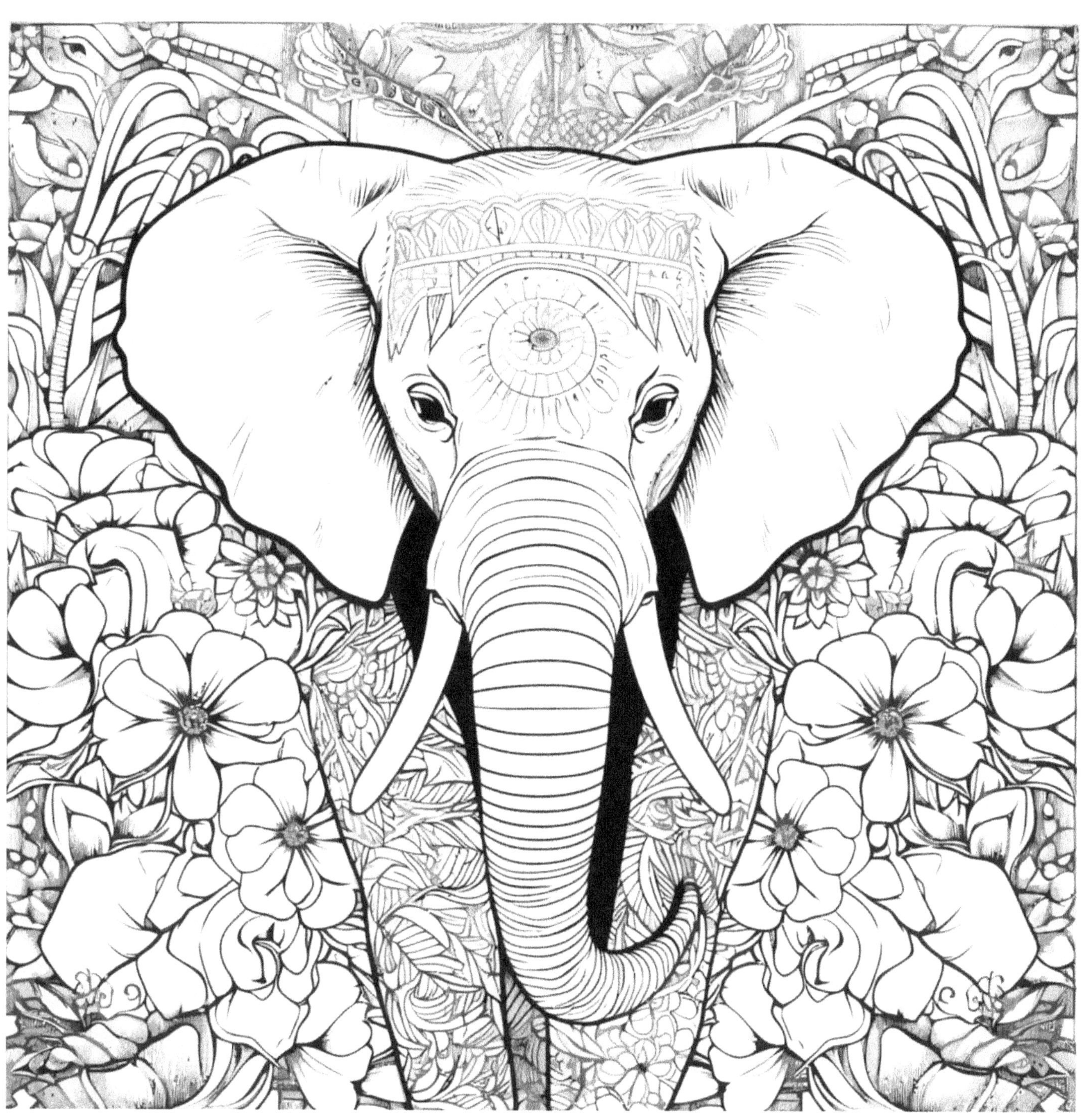

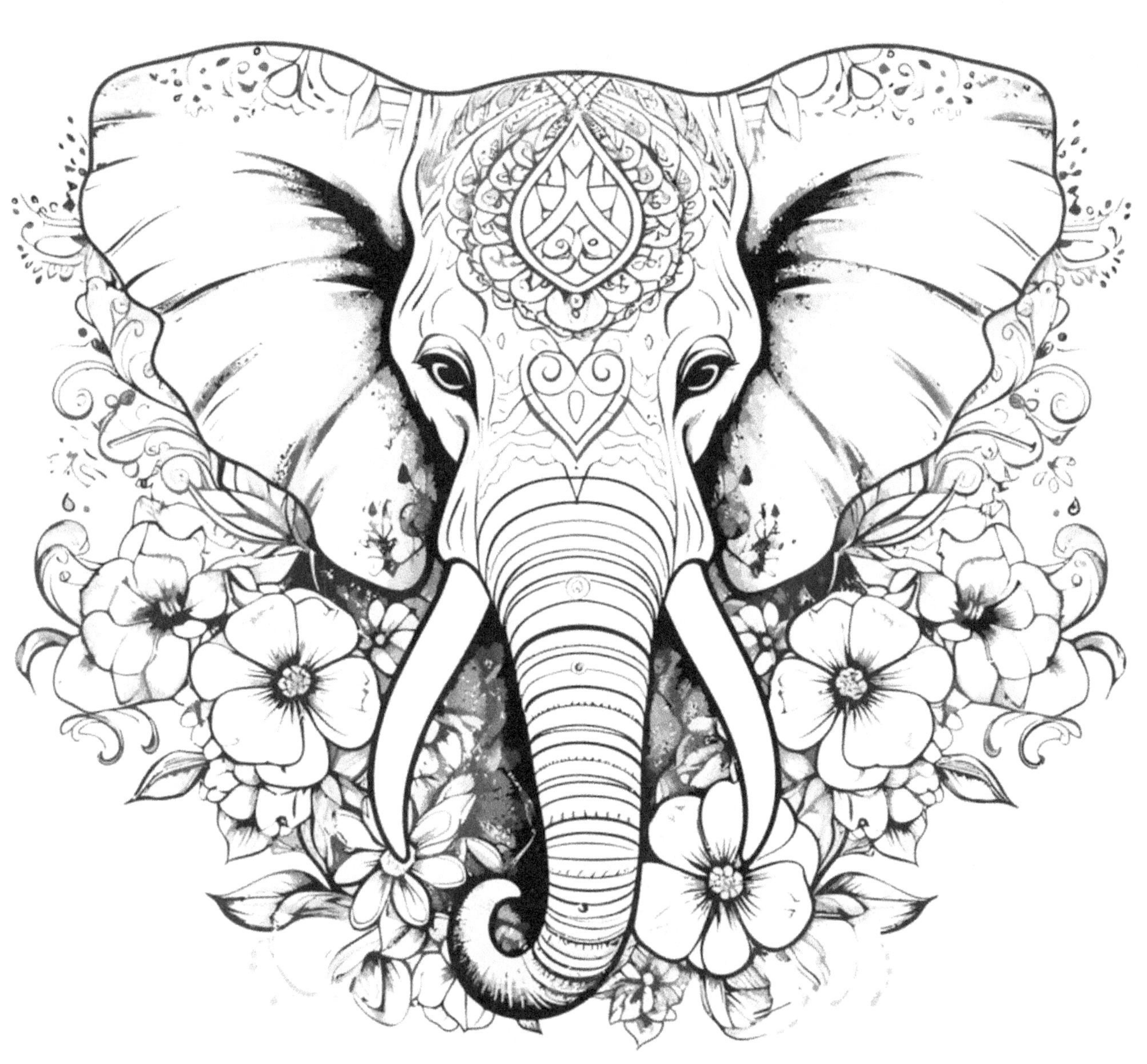

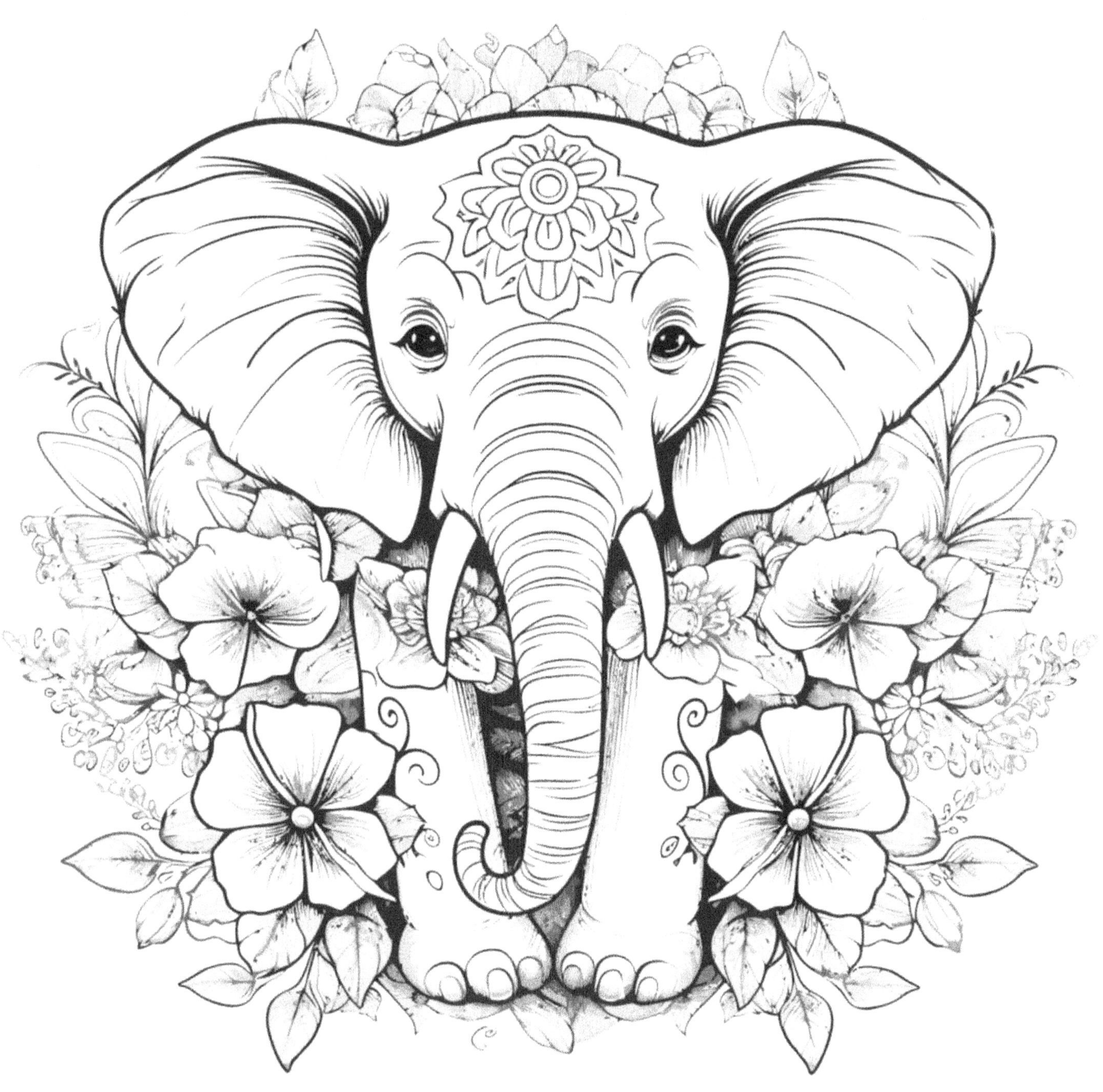

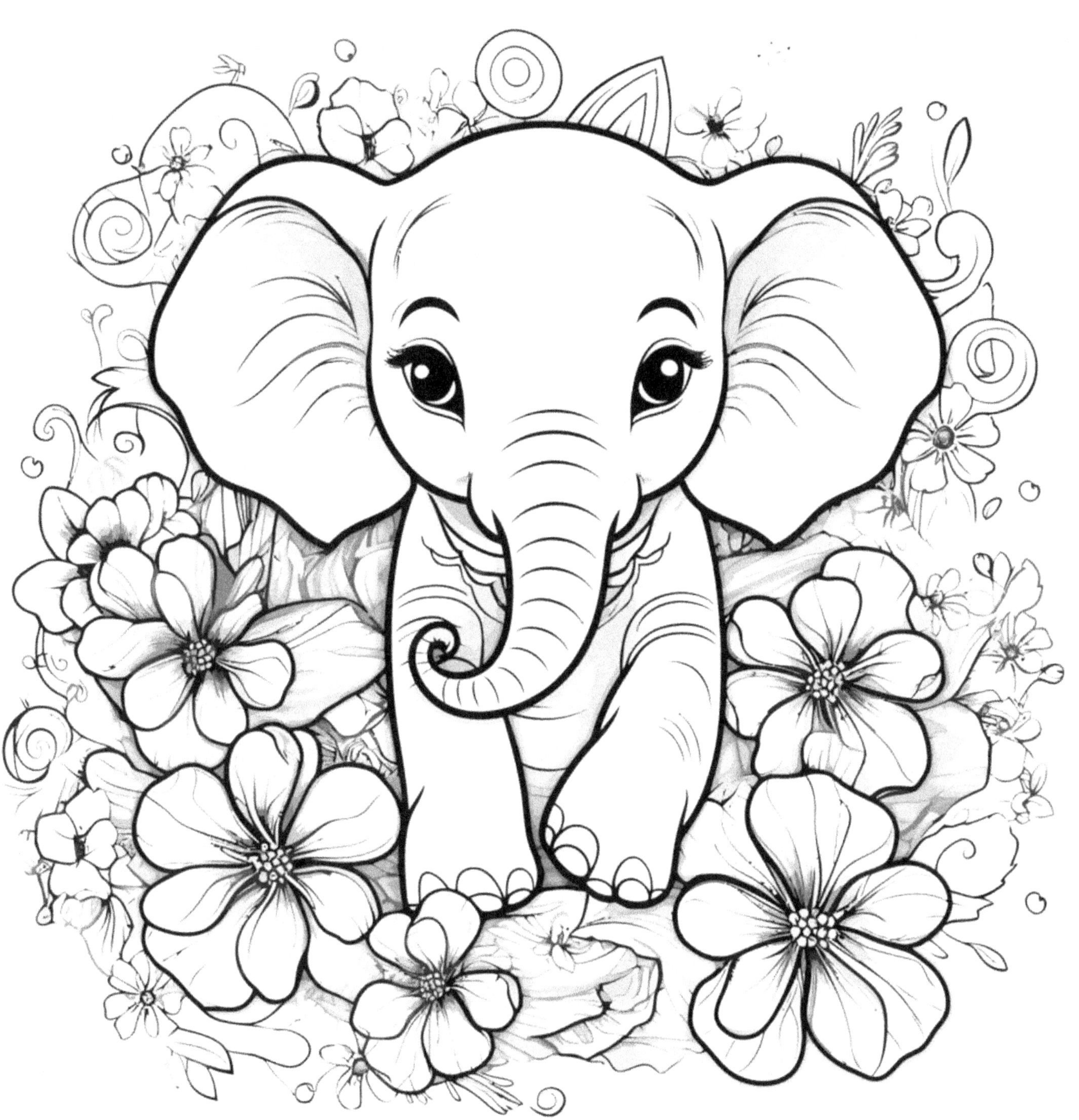

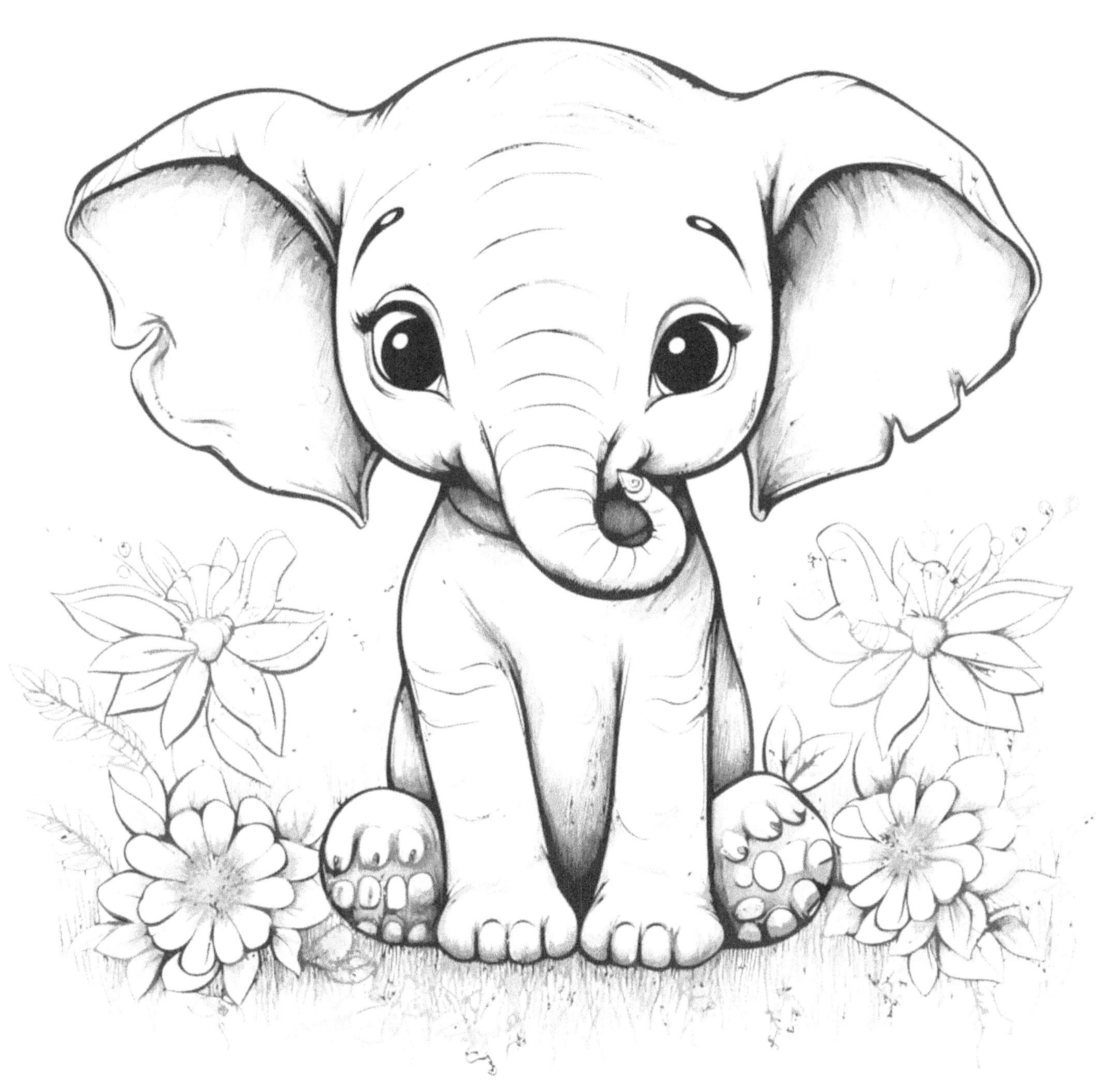

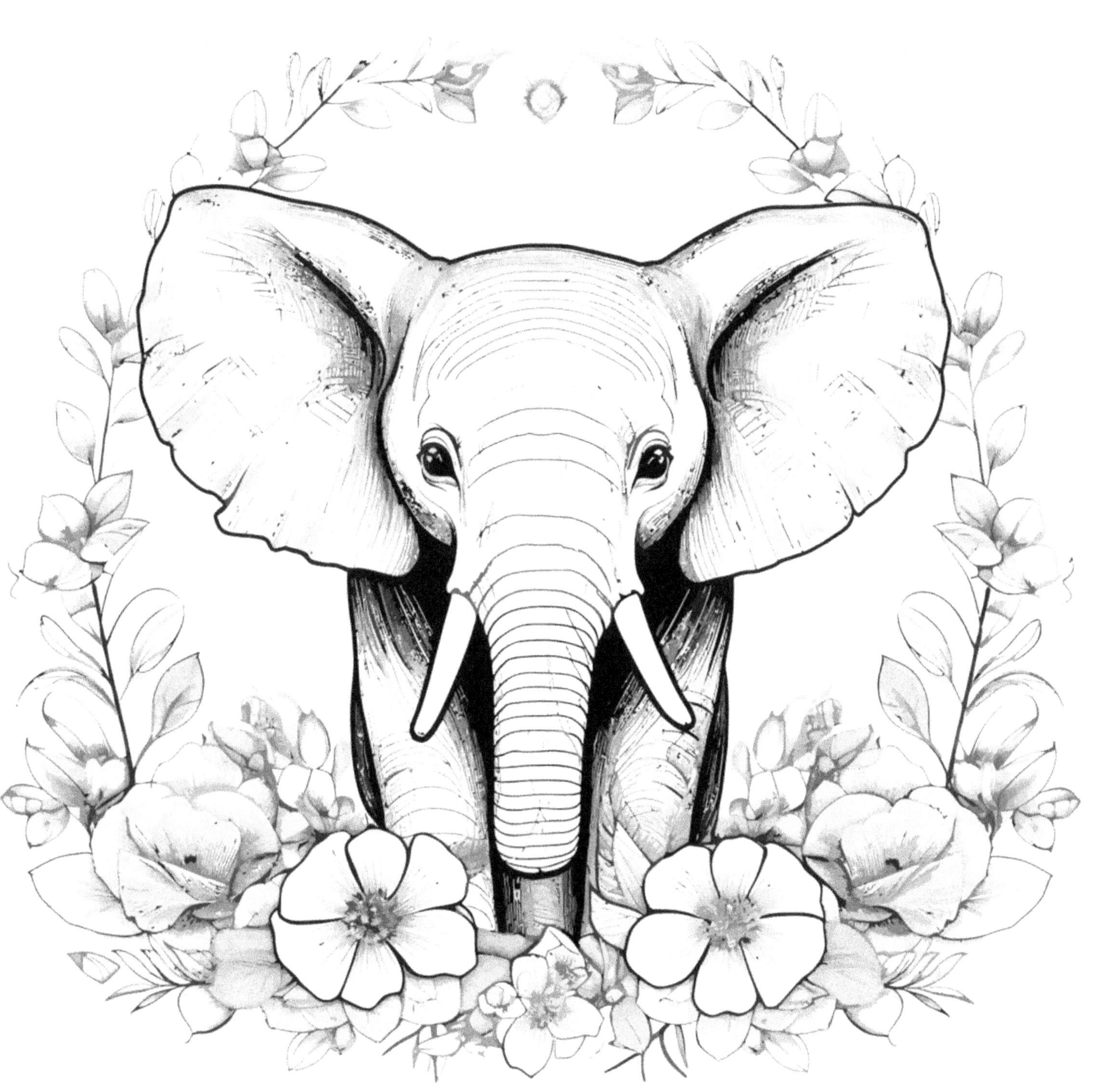

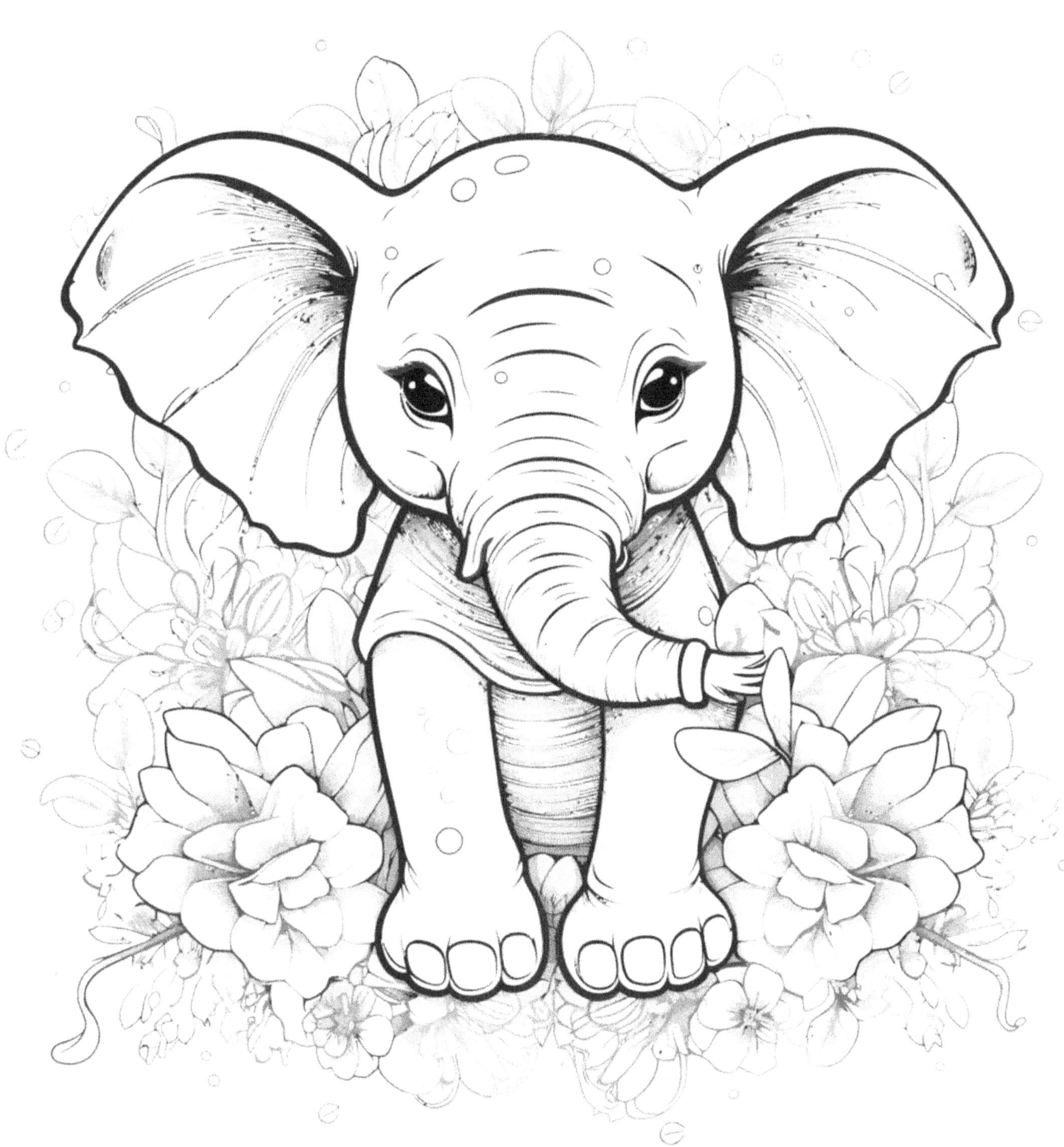

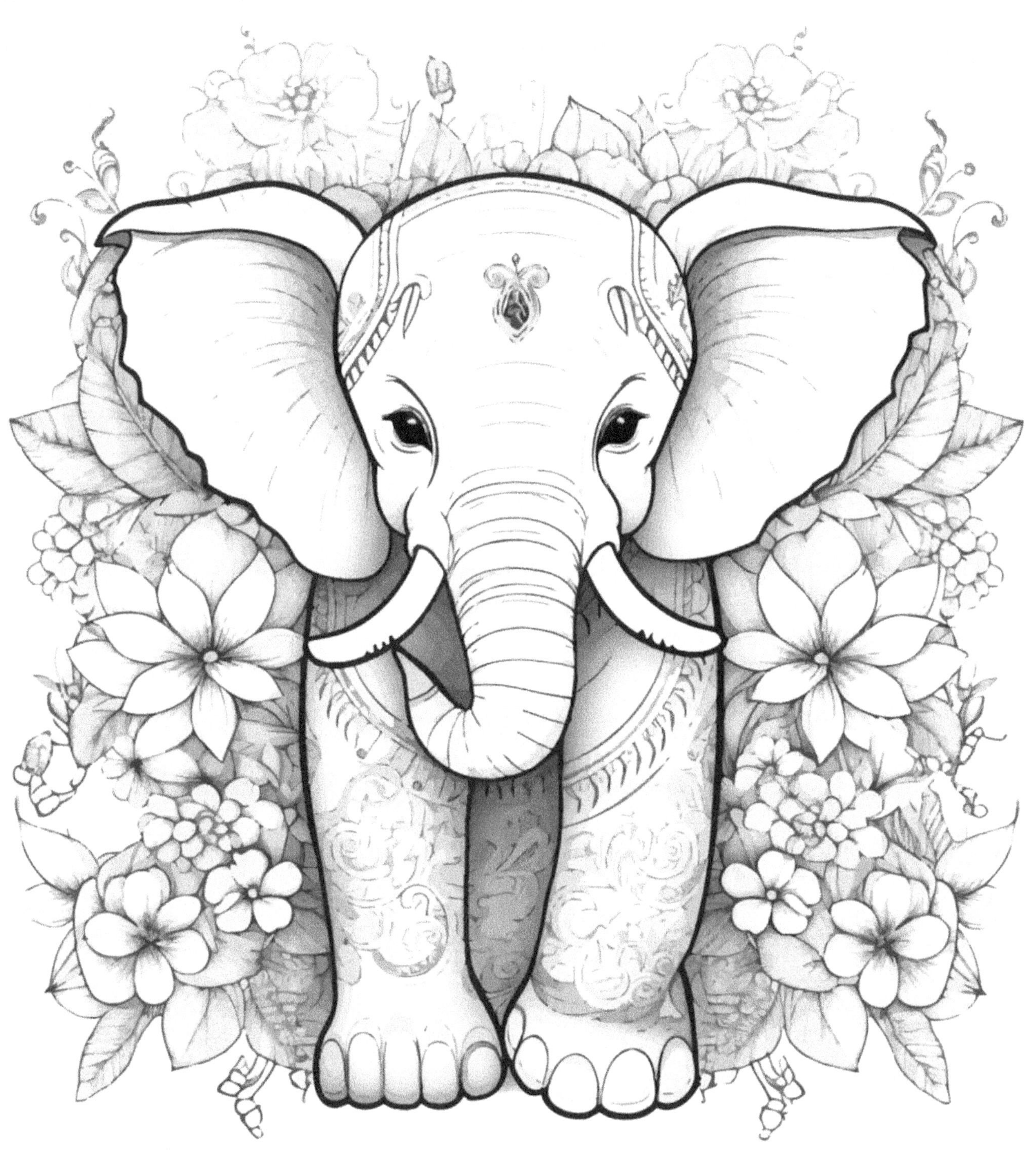

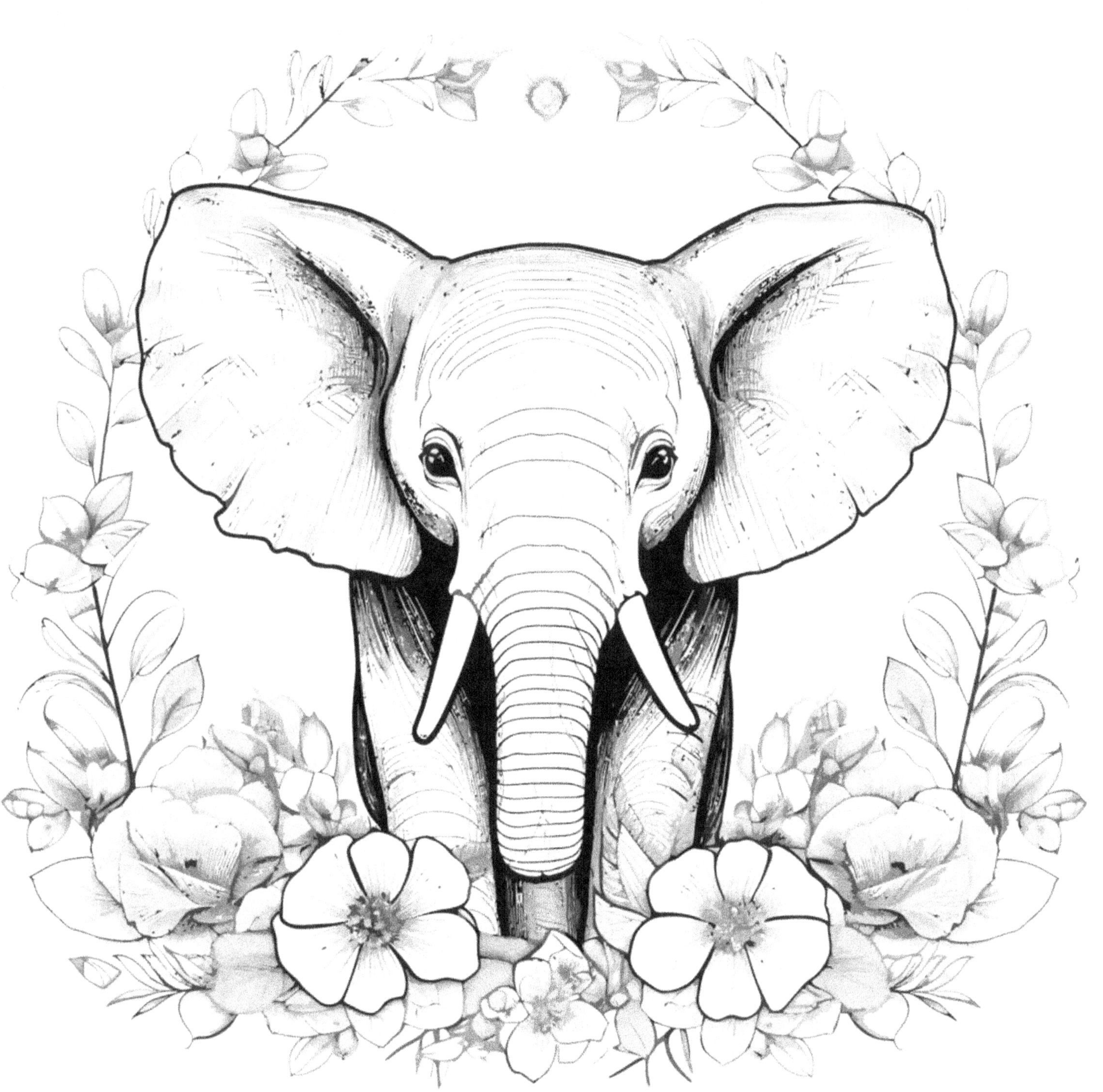

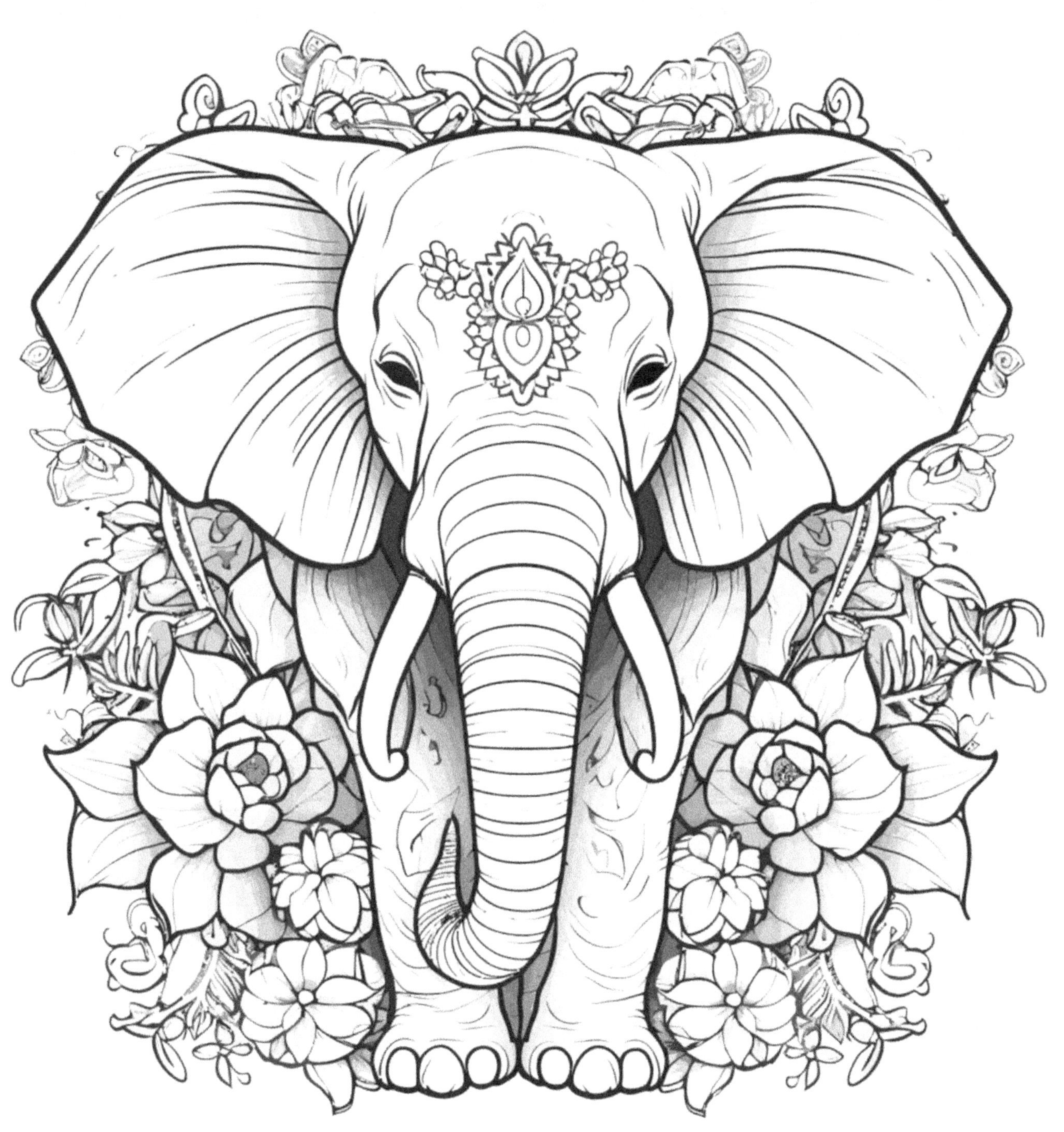

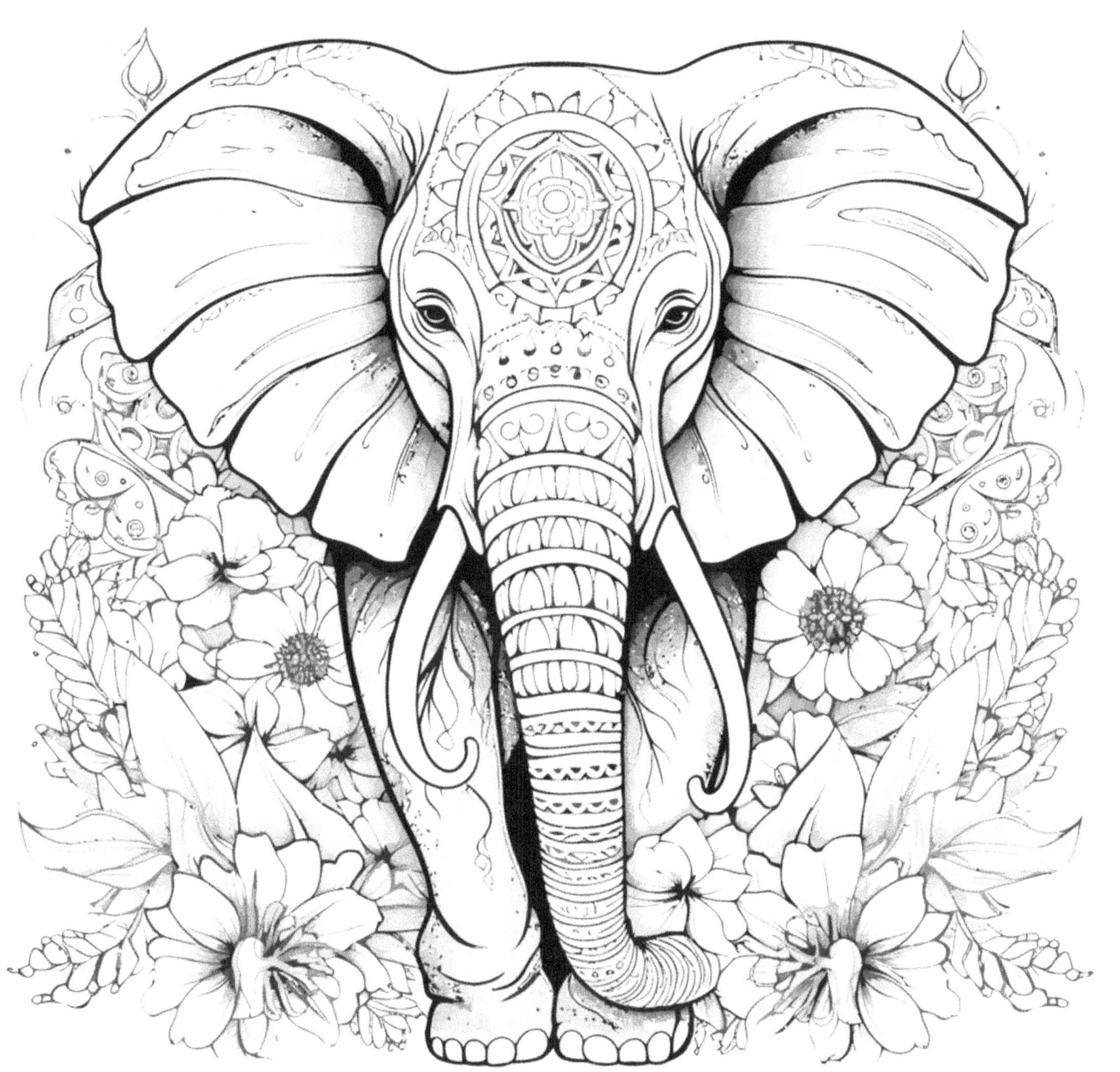

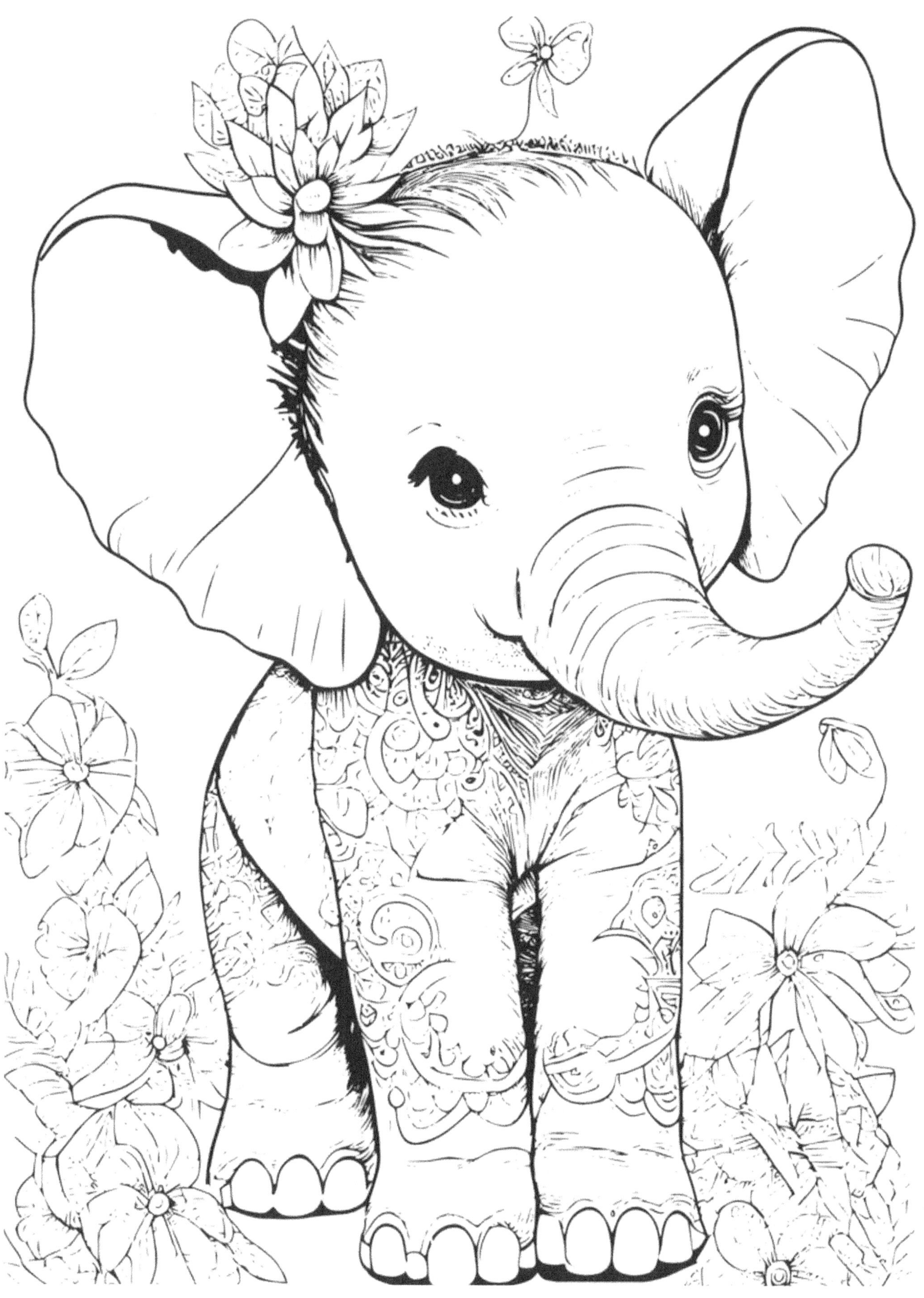

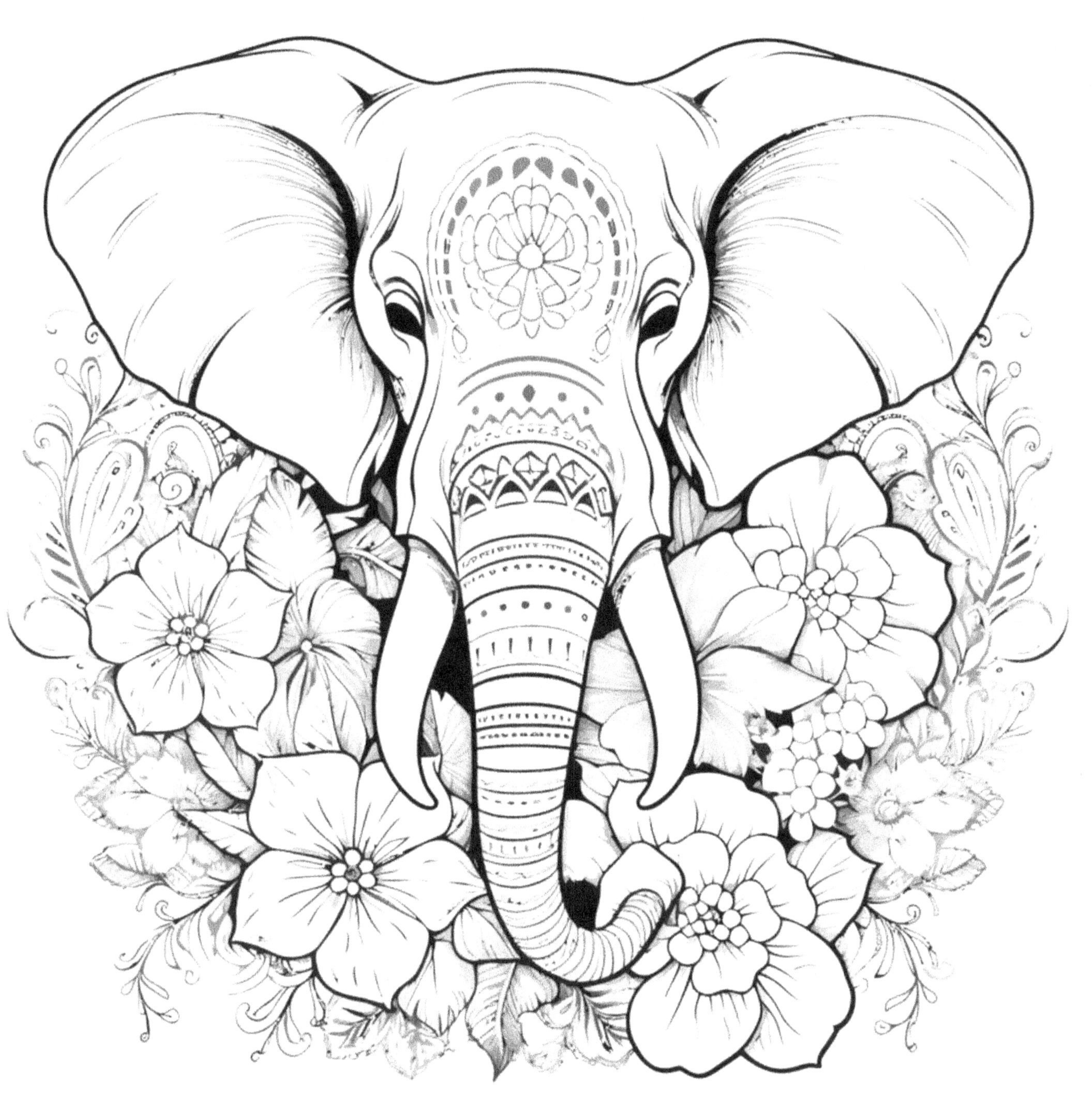

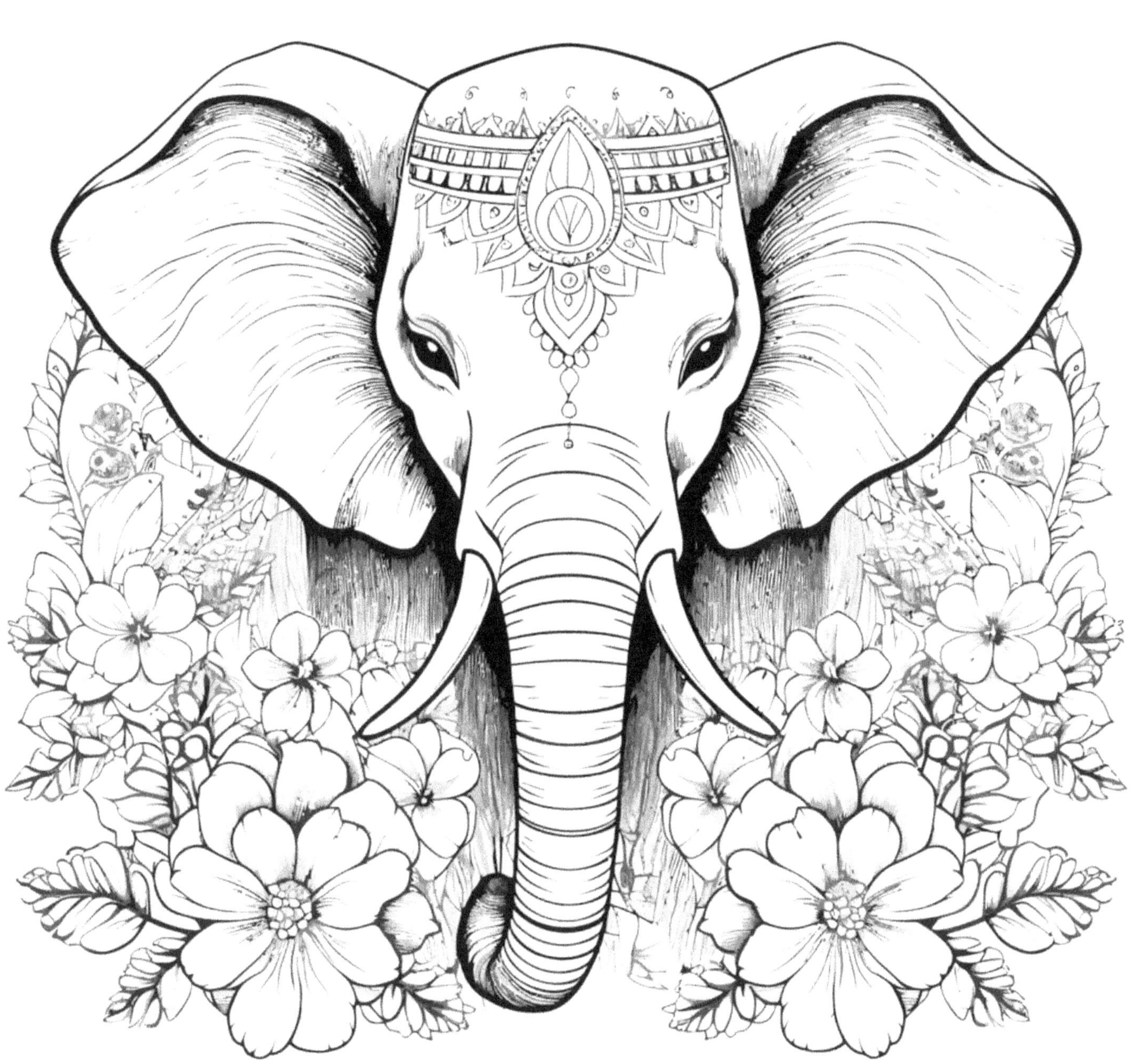

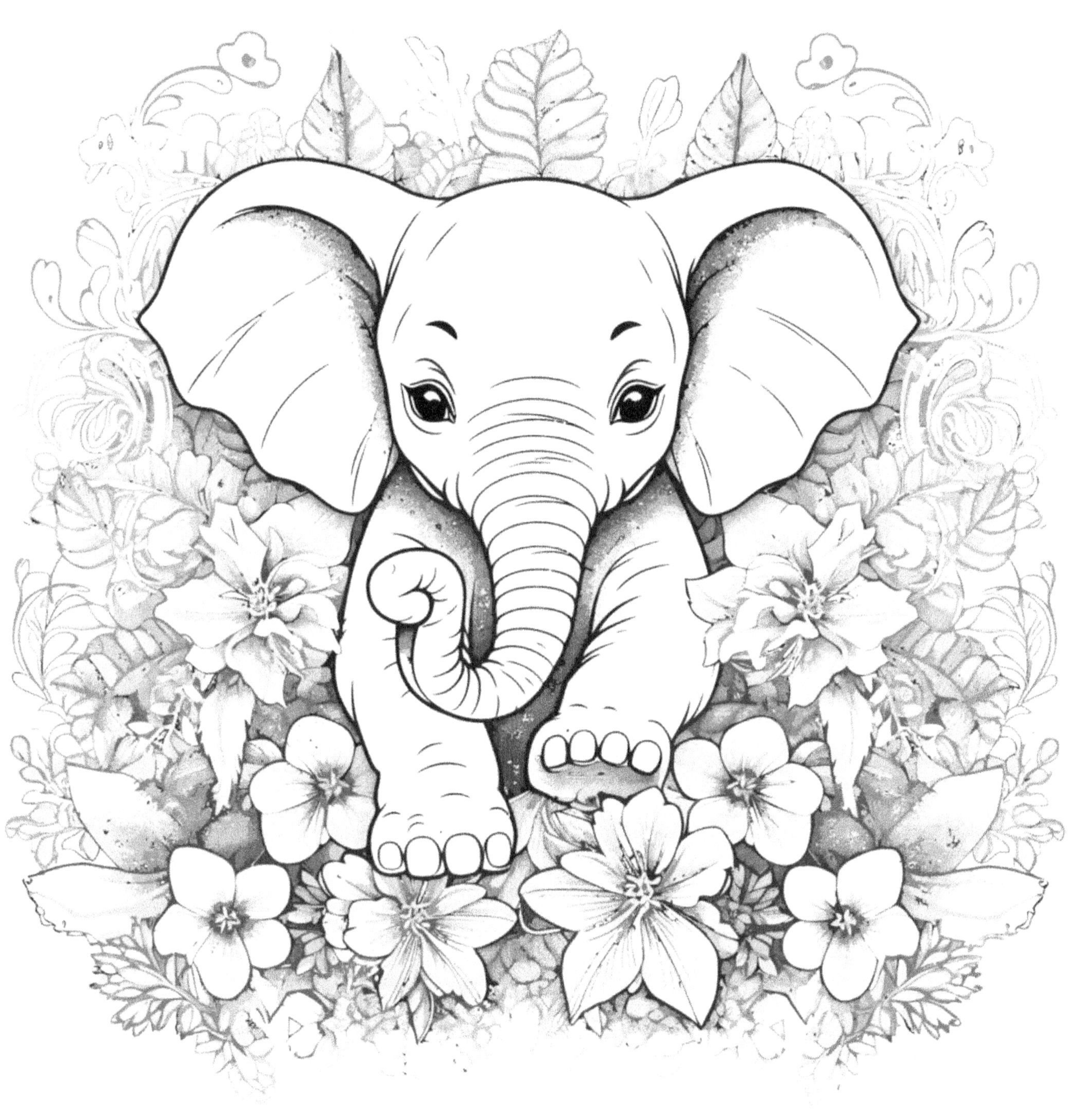

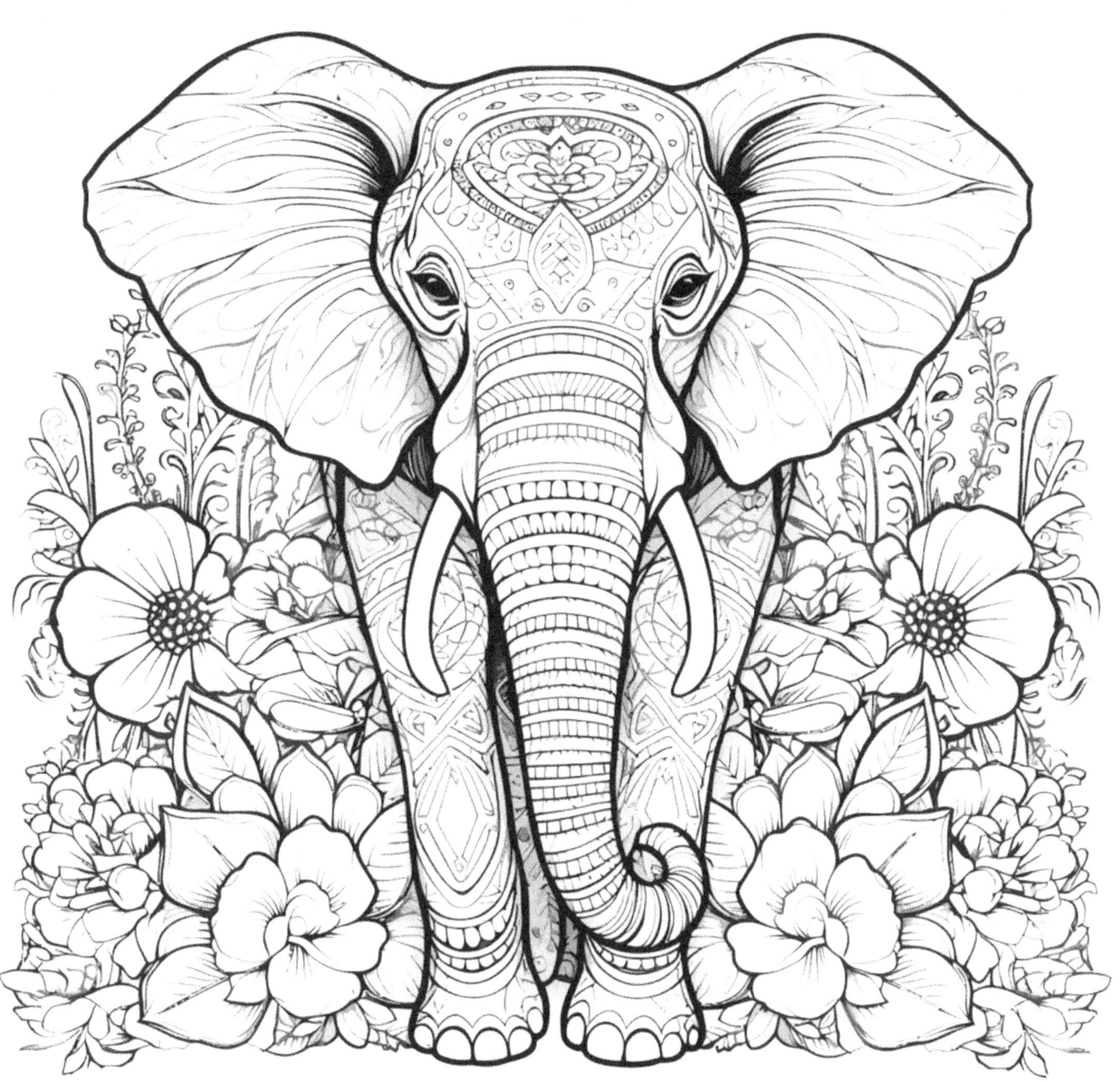

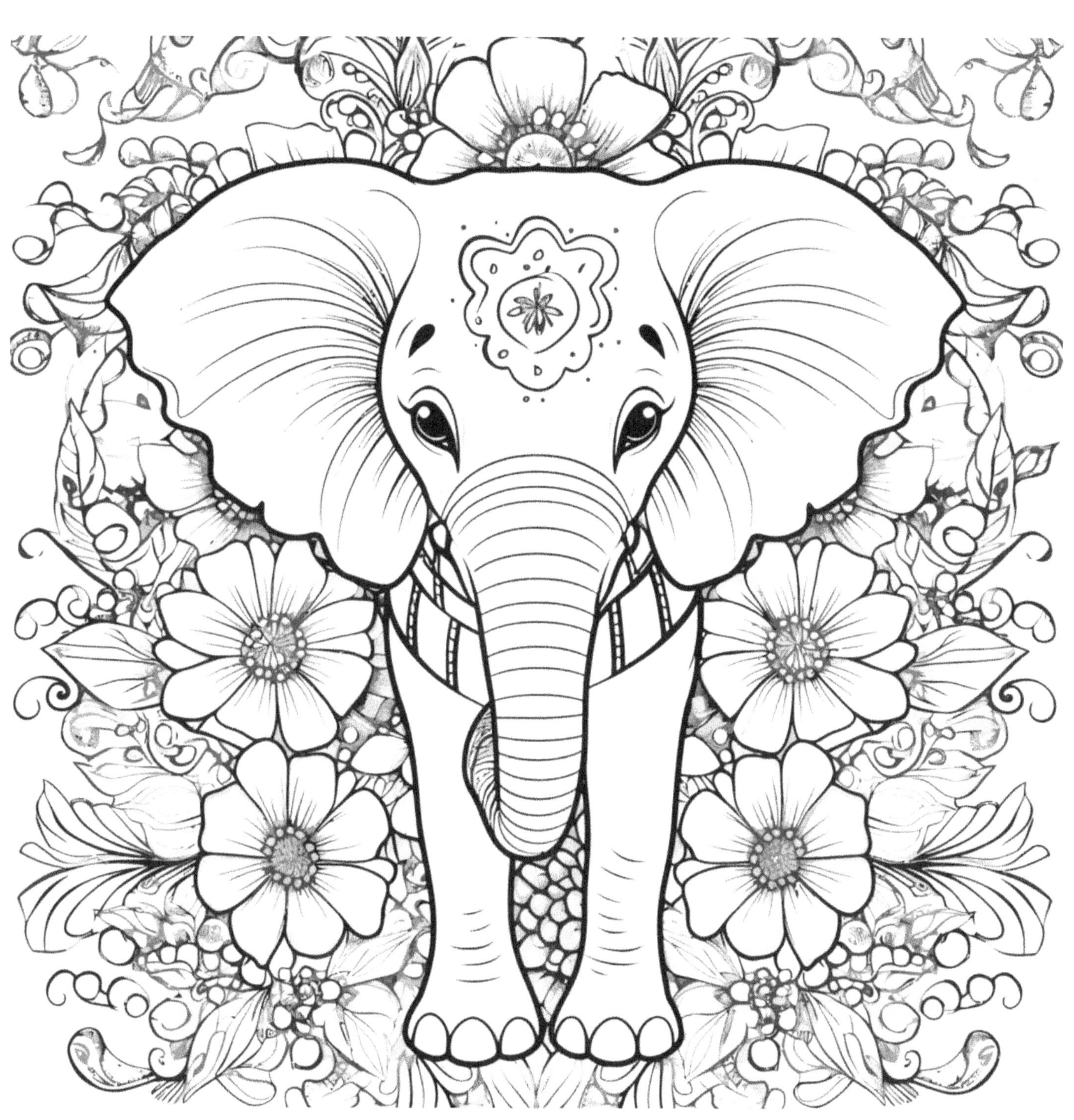

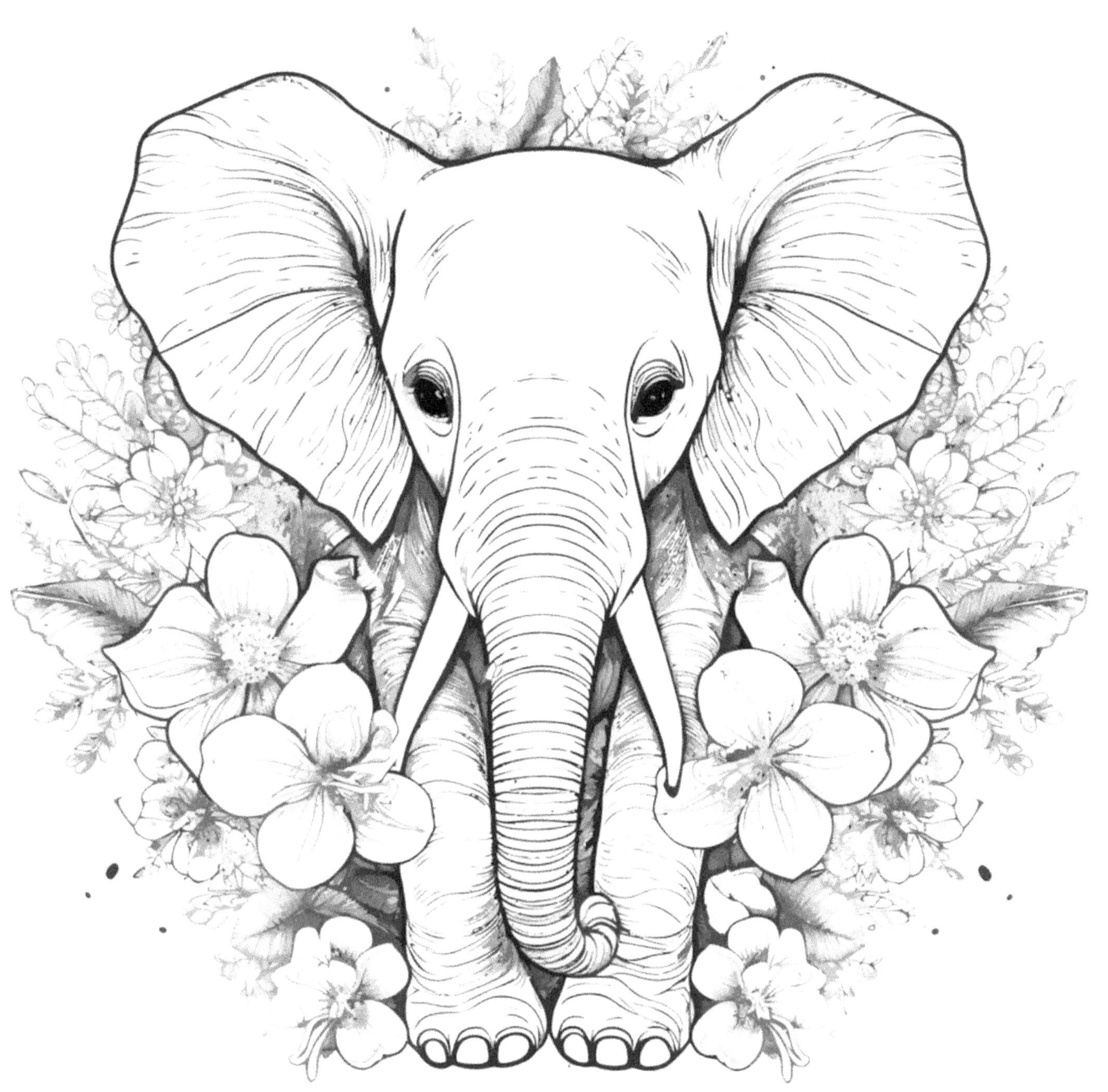

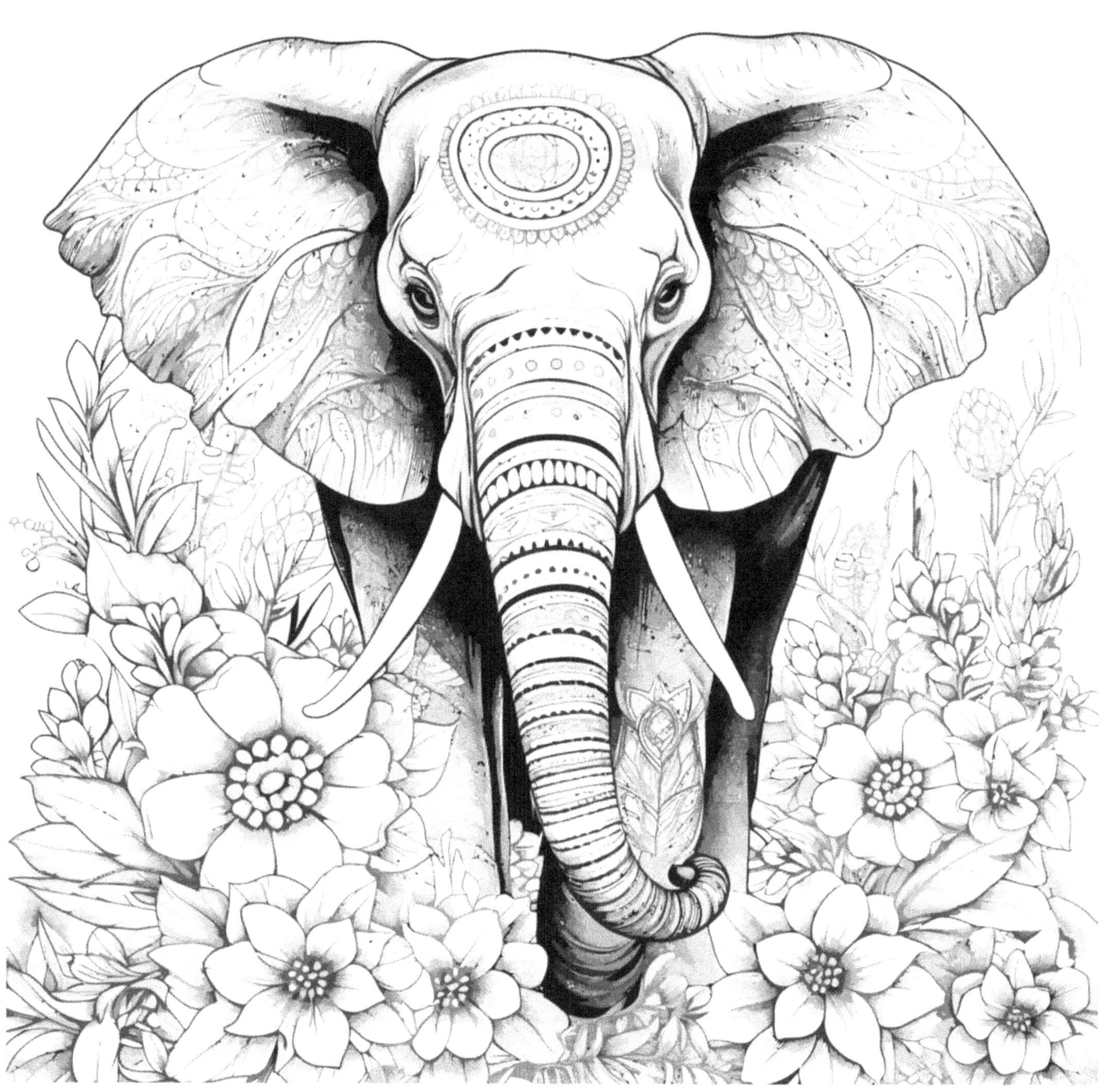

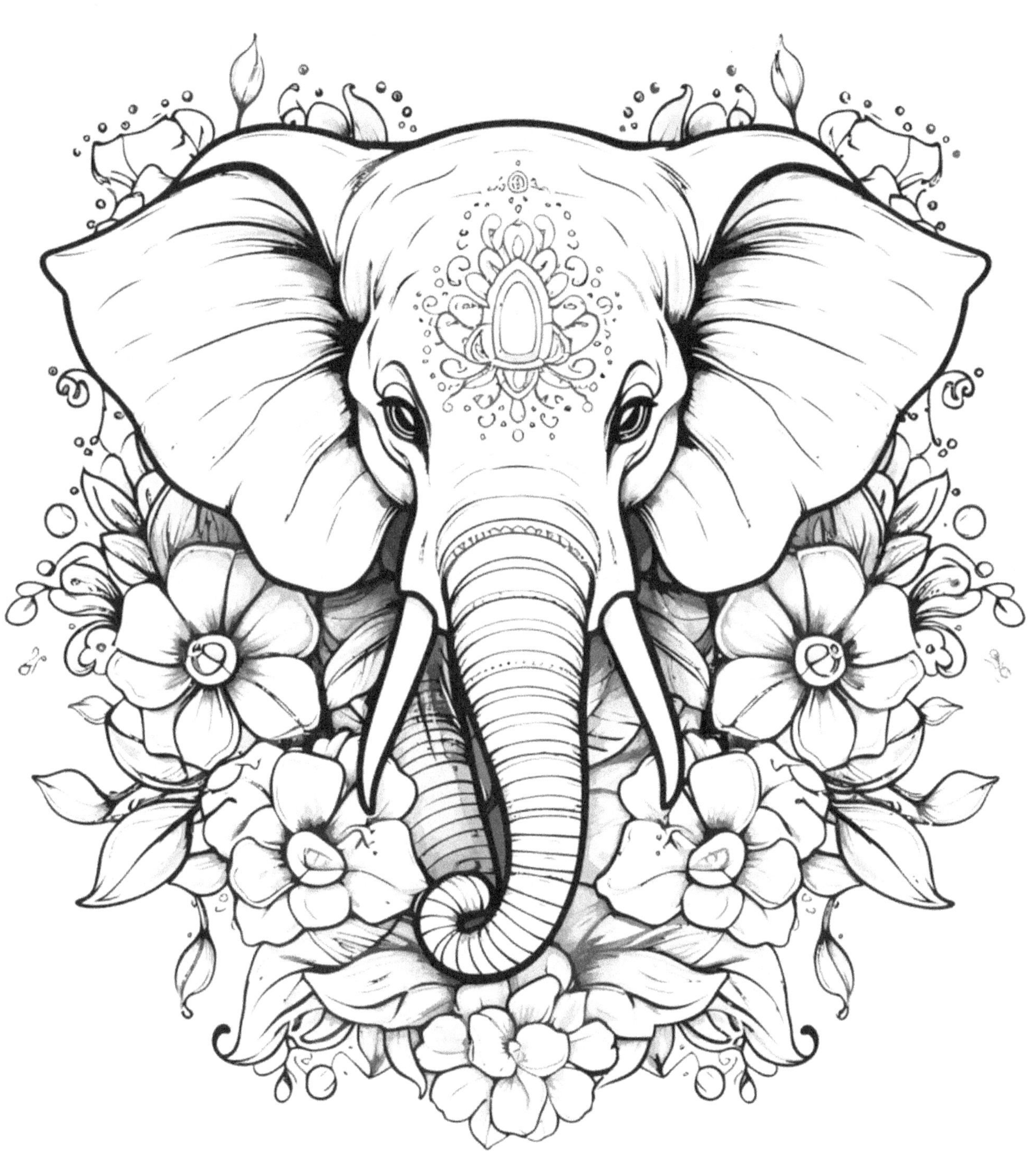

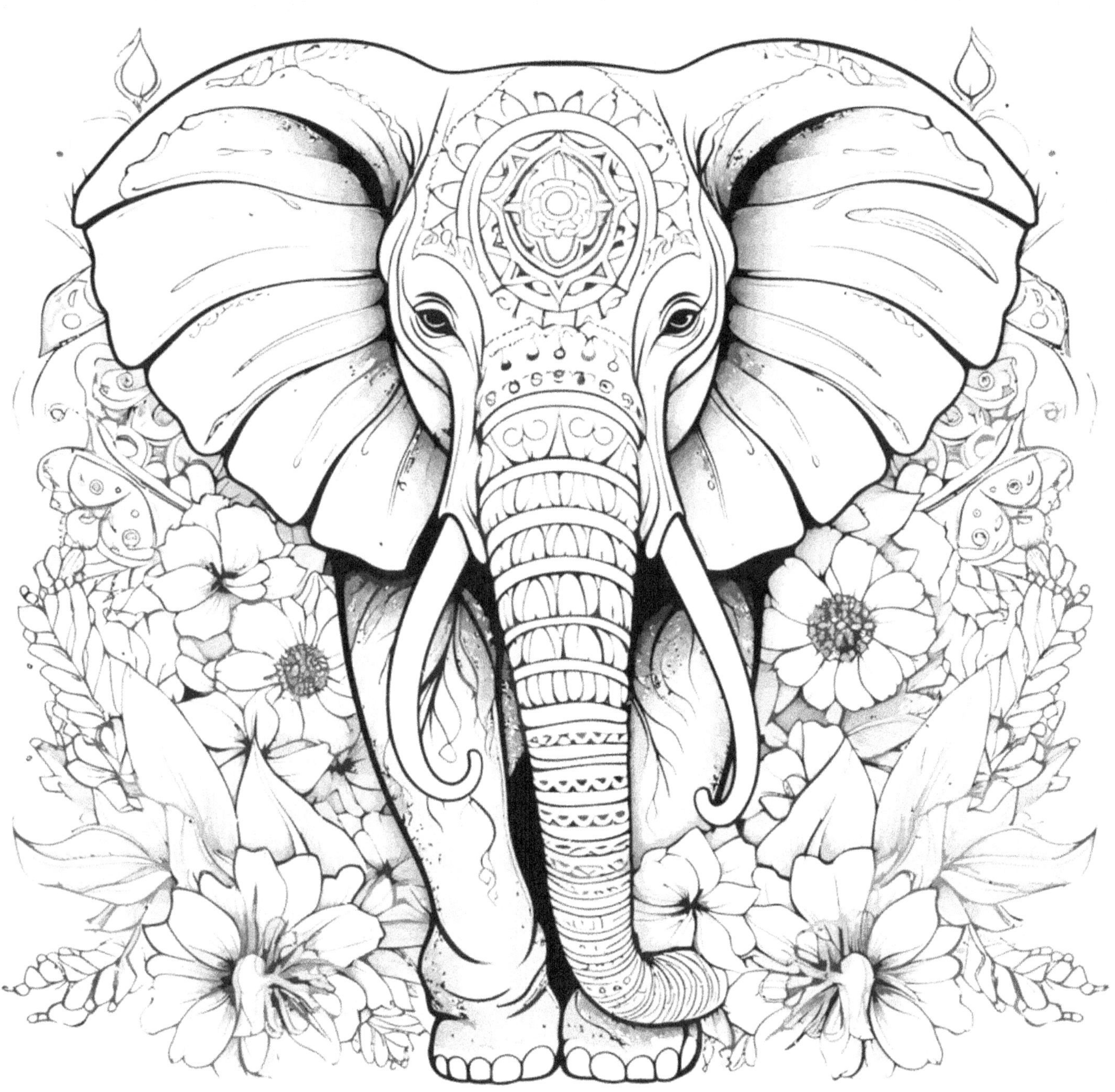

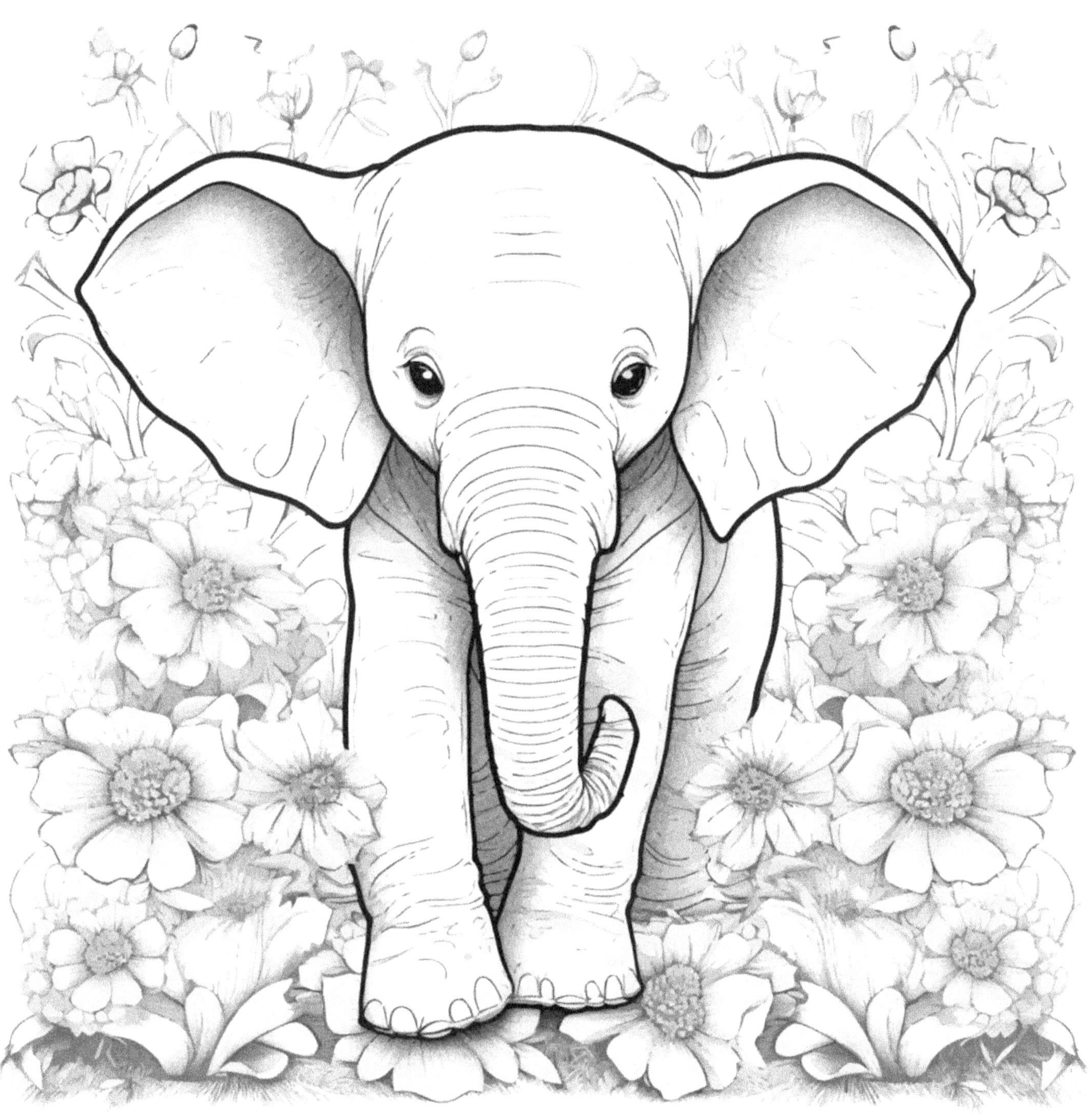